# The Seven Marriages
## of Your Marriage

# The Seven Marriages of Your Marriage

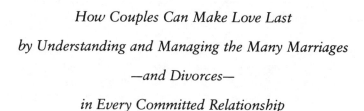

*How Couples Can Make Love Last
by Understanding and Managing the Many Marriages
—and Divorces—
in Every Committed Relationship*

Mel Krantzler, Ph.D.,
and
Patricia B. Krantzler, M.A.

HarperSanFrancisco
*A Division of* HarperCollins*Publishers*

Grateful acknowledgment is made to Penguin Books USA Inc. for permission to quote from D. H. Lawrence, "Being Alive" from *The Complete Poems of D. H. Lawrence,* copyright 1964, 1971 by Angelo Ravagli and C. M. Weekley, Executors of the Estate of Frieda Lawrence Ravagli and from "A Propos of Lady Chatterley's Lover," copyright 1930 by Frieda Lawrence, renewed © 1958 by the Estate of Frieda Lawrence Ravagli, from *Phoenix II: The Posthumous Papers of D. H. Lawrence* by D. H. Lawrence, edited by Roberts and Moore, used by permission of Viking Penguin, a division of Penguin Books USA Inc.; to Routledge, Chapman and Hall, Inc. for permission to quote from Bertolt Brecht, "When in My White Room at the Charité" from *Poems, 1913–56,* pp. 451–52; and to Susan Bergholz Literary Services, New York for permission to quote from "Good Taste," which originally appeared in *Ode to a Dodo: Poems 1953 to 1978,* copyright © 1981 by Christopher Logue, first published by Jonathan Cape Ltd., London.

FIRST EDITION

*Library of Congress Cataloging-in-Publication Data*

Krantzler, Mel.
    The seven marriages of your marriage : how couples can make love last by understanding and managing the many marriages—and divorces—in every committed relationship / Mel Krantzler, Patricia B. Krantzler. — 1st ed.
      p.    cm.
    ISBN 0–06–250633–1
    Includes bibliographic references and index.
    1. Marriage.   I. Krantzler, Patricia B.  II. Title.
HQ734.K87 1992                        91–58157
306.81—dc20                             CIP

92  93  94  95  96  HAD  10  9  8  7  6  5  4  3  2  1

This edition is printed on recycled, acid-free paper that meets the American National Standards Institute Z39.48 Standard.

# Contents

# Introduction

Our book invites you to rediscover your marriage so that you can mine the gold that exists within it. The following nine chapters combine to form the rediscovery road map that leads to long-term happiness and personal fulfillment for couples.

How is this possible when we live in a time when one out of every two couples will divorce? Although 95 percent of all adults marry at least once, 50 percent of these couples divorce, usually within seven years after the wedding. This is hardly an advertisement for marriage as a guarantee of long-term happiness. It is a statistic that offers ammunition to all of the millions of men and women who fear that given the doubling of our life spans since the beginning of the twentieth century, the possibility of remaining happily and faithfully married to the same person for many decades or even a lifetime is minimal at best.

This attitude implies that you and your partner are the "same" persons in the "same" marriage throughout the entire time you live together. Indeed, if this were true a couple would smother in the boredom of each other's unchanging personalities, in the dreary predictability of each additional year of marriage. You would simply be older, worn-out copies of who you were at the time you took out your marriage license.

However, our seventeen years' experience as marriage counselors affirms that this bleak picture of the marital condition need not be true! We have counseled thousands of couples in troubled relationships who have revitalized their lives together, rather than divorcing, by utilizing our unique approach to marriage, which reveals that instead of "one" marriage, every couple lives through many marriages throughout the years they spend together. In a lifetime together you experience seven marriages of your marriage, rather than one. Our approach enables couples to recognize those seven dramatically different marriages and the seven different ways of stretching themselves and relating to each other they need in order to weather the crises, the boredom, the taken-for-granteds, the hurt feelings, the misreading of each other's intentions that can occur in any committed relationship.

This book charts the ways you can identify and deal skillfully with your own seven marriages, so that you can welcome each of the marriages when it emerges and use it to enhance your relationship at whatever age or period in life you have reached. It should be noted that these seven developments in your marriage are not stages; their differences from one another are as profound as the differences you experienced when you first took out a marriage license and established a household together in place of being two single persons courting each other. In turn, these new marriages require new ways of relating to each other, which our book details so that you can fine-tune your relationship. Our approach applies to those who are considering marriage for the first time; to those who are in a second marriage, or hesitantly thinking of marrying again; to those who have never married and still have mixed feelings about taking the marriage step; to those who are in a living-together arrangement and fear that the next step of marriage would lead to a breakup; or to widows or widowers over fifty who have put life on permanent hold after a spouse has died.

We hope you will see your own relationship in a new light, a light that will empower you and your partner to reassess where you have been in the past as a couple, how you are currently relating, and where you will travel to in the next marriage of your marriage. The poet Emily Dickinson once wrote, "Hope is the thing with feathers," a beautiful image of hope as a bird soaring in flight. All of us need hope to sustain our lives in the present and to stretch ourselves toward the future. The courage to fly in marriage is the courage to re-create your marriage each time a new marriage of your marriage appears on the horizon of your relationship. Our book is designed to light the way for you and your partner so that long-term marital life becomes the loving, enriching connection we all have the right to expect it to be.

*Part One*

# The Happiness
# in the Journey

# Chapter One

# *Rediscovering Marriage*

It was a very special occasion. My wife, Pat, and I were celebrating our seventh wedding anniversary and were looking forward to a candlelight-and-wine dinner at a fine restaurant and then a show.

While Pat was getting ready, I sat on our living room sofa, and thoughts about our marriage started dancing in my mind:

Seven years! The number comedians had always made jokes about: "The seven-year itch, are you scratching yet? Are you itching to end your marriage? Ha, ha!" But maybe it was no laughing matter, for it is a fact that most divorces happen within seven years of the wedding.

Did I have that "itch" too? My answer was a resounding no! In fact our marriage, seven years into it, was more involving, more exciting, more enriching than it had ever been. It was getting better, not worse, as the years rolled on. Where did we go right? I wondered. Shouldn't our marriage be more on the boring side after seven years? Shouldn't we be taking each other for granted? After all, conventional wisdom has it that you "settle down" to marriage. That sounds like an unpleasant duty, as though once "the marriage knot is tied" you should forget about it and concentrate on more important things. And doesn't a knot that's tied imply that two people will strangle each other to death?

However, none of this applied to our marriage. Why not? I kept searching my mind for the answer: Why weren't we drifting in the direction that one out of every two marriages does, that is, downhill all the way to divorce?

Pat suddenly appeared, and my thoughts went on hold. I was caught up in the vision of her: She looked beautiful, alive, and glistening, not a pained reflection of a worn-out marriage. She did not look the same as she did when we married. I found her very attractive then, but now even more so; she was more self-reliant, more mature. She had changed! I was so surprised at this discovery that I blurted out, "Pat, you've changed, you're not the same person I married!"

Here is Pat's narration of what happened next:

I remember Mel had an astonished look on his face when he blurted out to me, "You've changed, you're not the same person I married!" To me it was like a slap in the face. It startled me, because I was looking forward to a grand evening. To walk into the room and be struck with those words just knocked the props from under me. I became very defensive and said to him, "Hey, that's not true, I'll always be the same girl you married." You see, I automatically assumed that change was something bad, that it meant the other person wouldn't be interested in you. Change to me always meant a threatened relationship. I thought he was trying to tell me he no longer wanted to be married to me, and that frightened me. I was going to reassure him I hadn't changed, that the core of me that he fell in love with was still there, so why would he make a derogatory statement like that? I kept insisting I still was the same person he married.

Mel then quickly reassured me that he was complimenting me when he said I had changed. "You see, Pat, I've been sitting here thinking about our marriage," he said. "It's not bad that you or I have changed. In fact, it's wonderful—it stimulates our marriage. Change makes our marriage much better than it was at the beginning because so many different parts of ourselves have emerged since we married, making us so much more interesting to each other."

Both of us felt we were discovering something very important about change in our own marriage and continued to pursue this idea during dinner. Now that I knew Mel was not putting me down but praising me when he said I had changed, I began to see clearly the changes in my own life in the first seven years of our marriage.

At the time I met Mel I was a secretary and office manager with two teenage daughters. I had been a traditional housewife who left college after two semesters to marry my first husband and had stayed home most of the time to raise our children. After all, that was what society insisted married women do back in the 1950s. Now here I was seven years into my second marriage, a college graduate rather than a dropout. I no longer believed that women were second-best to men and had established a "two-getherness" relationship with Mel, a marriage of two equals in which we respected and reinforced each other's individual growth as well as our growth as a couple. My two girls were now married, and we shared adult-to-adult friendships in addition to a parent-to-child bond. I was now beginning a career as a psychologist. Seven years earlier, I had worked at "jobs"; now I worked at a "career." Death had entered my life the previous year when my father, who was in his eighties, died, and that experience had helped me to see life as a journey with a beginning and an end.

But what about the journey most people take in their lives? Do they hold on to the belief that "I'll always be the same—I'll never change," as I once did? What are the changes we all go through in a marriage, and are we really aware that each and every day of our lives we are growing and changing? And what about our marriage? It had changed because we both had grown and stretched ourselves. When I worked in offices, I felt OK about my position as a secretary, but today it would no longer feel right. What are the changes of life? What are the changes in a marriage?

I remember that my mom and dad always looked with favor at the changes I made as a child. They applauded the various stages: kindergarten to first grade, middle school, high school, junior college, marriage, children. But then it seemed that I was no longer expected to grow and change, and the applause ended. It seems to me that it's assumed that once you marry and have children it's time to stop. Perhaps that's the very reason that marriages get into trouble.

Reviewing those seven years held a great surprise for me: I had changed in so many ways I was not aware of, and the changes were all for the better—both for me and for my marriage! Mel had applauded all my growth spurts, and for that I'm thankful.

After Pat shared these reflections with me, I started to total up the changes in my own life since we married: When I met Pat, I was working at a boring job in a state bureaucracy that would eventually destroy the soul of anyone working there. Pat encouraged me to quit my job and risk spreading my wings by starting a new career as the innovator of divorce counseling. Seven years later I was the director of our Creative Divorce, Love & Marriage Counseling Center, and Pat was the co-director. I had never written a book before I married Pat. But here I was, seven years into our marriage, and with Pat's help I had written two best-sellers, *Creative Divorce* and *Learning to Love Again*. I, too, had had two teenage daughters when we married. Now they were adults who were married, and I had a new adult-to-adult relationship with them. When I married Pat, I still held the idea that the man was the king of his marriage castle. Seven years later I had eliminated this demeaning attitude in myself and become instead a very public, very vocal advocate for complete gender equality at home and in the workplace.

My God! the changes we both had gone through in the seven years of our marriage! And then I caught myself: Did I say "our marriage"? I asked Pat when I shared these thoughts with her. "That's not right," I continued. "You and I haven't had 'one' marriage; we've already had more than one, a new marriage after seven years. Not only have we changed, our relationship has changed, our marriage has changed."

We both began to realize that if we had remained the "same" persons in the "same" marriage that we had been seven years previously we probably would have bored each other to death by now—and the seven-year itch would have infected both of us. Instead, our marriage had become an exciting adventure. It would be boring only if we did not change and we continued to take each other for granted. When marriage is understood to be an ongoing, developing series of changes in which two people can grow as individuals and as an interdependent couple, change can be welcomed rather than feared.

Since that seventh anniversary we have used the concept that there are many marriages in any long-term relationship to help the couples who come to us for counseling enliven the quality of their relationships rather than choose divorce. It is this concept and our experiences in helping each couple apply this concept to their own marriage that is the subject of this book.

With this perspective, marriage today becomes the catalyst for individual and couple growth within a relationship, rather than a way station on the road to divorce. The new relationship realities of today amount to a rediscovery of marriage, and we invite you to rediscover your marriage in this book so that life together becomes a continuous source of love and personal fulfillment. Here are the components of that rediscovery, which we call the emerging relationship revolution:

1. All surveys asking the question, How is it best to spend one's life? indicate that a happy marriage and family life rank at the very top of the list. The old, cynical, self-centered, what's-in-it-for-me attitude toward marriage seems to be disappearing. Taking its place is a view of marriage as an egalitarian, shared, lifetime experience. Significantly, the pursuit of money and of sex without love and commitment rank at the bottom of these surveys.

2. The divorce rate is declining while the marriage rate consistently remains at least double the divorce rate. This is an affirmation by both men and women that marriage is the best road to happiness—that they want love, companionship, understanding, respect, helpfulness, and caring in place of the sexual warfare of recent decades. The basic values of commitment—love, monogamy, teamwork, sacrifice, empathy, patience, loyalty, tenderness, kindness, consideration, compromise, and forgiveness—have been rediscovered and reaffirmed as the necessary building blocks for any happy marriage. Today, these values are freely chosen as values to live by instead of being espoused in theory but violated in practice, as they often were in past decades.

3. Seeking the services of a marriage counselor when unresolved marital conflicts arise (rather than allowing them to fester or ignoring them in the hope that time will make them

disappear) is now viewed as a sign of personal strength rather than of weakness. Couples who love each other are enabled to resolve their problems rather than remaining caught in the belief that they would rather be right than happy, an attitude that congeals into divorce. Couples no longer wait until a marriage sours to come to counseling: they come if they are considering marriage or if they have problems in a living-together arrangement. Lesbians and gays are also seeking marriage counseling for the difficulties they may experience, since they too live in committed relationships.

4. The two-career (or two-job) marriage is the primary economic form of marriage in today's times. (Even Blondie of comic strip fame has taken an outside job—after sixty-one years as a housewife!) The problems arising from this reality must be solved by each couple, with society's support—for example, how household chores and parenting demands will be shared, how to find adequate child care, how to resolve competitiveness and family power struggles. New public policies must be created also—new arrangements to ease family stress, such as flex-time, shared jobs, family leave time, and an end to unemployment. Political activity to attain these goals has become a necessity for creating a happy marriage.

5. Toleration for alternative marital arrangements is built into the structure of our society now that "Ozzie and Harriet" families account for less than 10 percent of all families in the United States. The variations in household composition include childless marriages; serial monogamous marriages; remarriages; never-married single-parent households; bisexual marriages; domestic-partner relationships; joint and sole custody parenting households; and long-term, monogamous, living-together

arrangements. Our society now permits the pragmatic test: if the arrangement is freely agreed to and contributes to the mutual happiness of the persons involved, any of these arrangements is "workable."

6. Although many different types of "marriages" are now "workable," all have one essential element in common: They are all "two-gether" marriages or relationships, in contrast to the old stereotyped "together" form of marriage in which it was believed that a couple had to think, act, and feel the same in order to be successfully married. The new two-gether marriage acknowledges that a happy marriage comprises two equal partners; both believe they are treating each other fairly and that differences can enhance their relationship rather than diminish it.

7. The relationship revolution focuses attention on improving the quality of marital life rather than ending a stressful marriage in a legal divorce. It asks the fundamental question, Do you want a divorce, or a new marriage of your marriage? Would you and your partner rather divorce yourselves from self-defeating behaviors than divorce yourselves from each other? Would you rather have a closer, more loving relationship instead of breaking up?

8. The relationship revolution is reinforced by the new adult age revolution, which supports couples in renewing and reinvigorating their marriages at any age. This revolution is shattering all previous conceptions of how one's chronological age should control one's self-image, beliefs, attitudes, behavior, and expectations throughout life. We are no longer pressured by society's demand that we go to college at a particular time, stay in one career throughout a lifetime, retire in our fifties and sixties, and succumb to the belief that life is a downhill slide after forty.

Married couples now have the opportunity to make marriage a greater source of excitement and happiness by connecting with this new adult age revolution, which affirms that you can grow and change for the better, separately as well as together, throughout an entire lifetime. The only stopping time is death.

9. Divorce is now becoming a last resort, rather than a first resort. Though it is now an option acceptable to society and to most churches, it is being chosen more sparingly and thoughtfully than in previous decades. The idea that all problems would be solved by divorce turned out to be a painful illusion. If divorce must occur, there are many support systems now available for divorced men and women (e.g., divorce groups, church counseling, continuing education divorce courses). The modern psychological findings that divorce can become a new opportunity for personal growth—painful as it may be—bring hope rather than devastation to the million-plus couples who divorce each year. However, that hope requires taking personal responsibility for establishing a new way of life. To achieve happiness through divorce requires far greater effort than trying to create a happy new marriage of your marriage instead.

10. A far greater degree of empathy and understanding now exists between men and women. Men are striving to become more fully human by getting in touch with all sides of their personalities. Groups popularized by authors such as Robert Bly give men an opportunity to explore and share their lives. Men are taking a cue from women's support groups about how they, too, can benefit from destroying old male-female stereotypes that perpetuate hostility between the sexes. And now that the majority of women are sharing in the challenges and adversities of the working world to which men have always been exposed, an empathy is being forged between the sexes.

# The Seven Marriages of Your Marriage: The Keys to Personal Happiness

The new realities of this emerging relationship revolution can function as the take-off points for a lifetime of marital happiness only when they are applied with the knowledge that a lifetime marriage consists of seven marriages of your marriage rather than one. Imagine how utterly boring it would be if every couple were doomed to live together for forty or more years in the "same" way, believing marriage to be a set of routines and behaviors that remains unchanged. Unfortunately, too many couples still live in this way, unaware that they can choose to enliven their marital life by embarking on a new "marriage" in their marriage. This is the choice we are presenting to you here. You can begin to take advantage of the excitement and challenges that inhere in your marriage once you become aware of the existence of those seven marriages.

In this first chapter we will identify the seven marriages. Subsequent chapters will demonstrate the techniques you can apply to enhance and revitalize your couple relationship as you move through the seven marriages.

## 1. The Movie-Marriage-in-Your-Mind Marriage

In the first few years of marriage you begin to discover that your everyday lives together clash with your expectations, expectations derived from what you absorbed from your parents' marriage, from the media, from the culture you grew up in, and expectations developed from not seeing who your partner really is. The movie-marriage-in-your-mind, this clash of expectations with reality, causes there to be more divorces in the first few years than at any other period in marital life.

## 2. The Our-Careers-Are-Everything Marriage

Once you survive the movie-marriage-in-your-mind, your focus shifts to struggling up the career ladder. In the our-careers-are-everything marriage, the emphasis turns to laying the groundwork for stabilizing your life in a good job, so that you can accumulate material goods, savings, and a decent home. For the majority of couples today, this means adjusting to the demands of a two-career (or two-job) marriage; the old division of labor that was the rule for most of our parents—the husband as sole "provider" and the wife as mother and homemaker—is now the exception.

## 3. The Good-Enough-Parent Marriage

Childless marriages are still the exception. The modern trend is to have one or two children and to have them later in one's marriage, once careers are stabilized. The same couples who in their twenties insisted they would "never" have children usually change their minds in their thirties or early forties. These couples struggle with the difficulties and risks of getting pregnant and with decisions about adoption.

## 4. The Time-Is-Running-Out Marriage

In the late thirties and early forties you recognize the need to focus on the quality of your life, because your time on earth is limited. Witnessing the severe illness and/or death of some of your loved ones or friends or acquaintances who are no older than you (increasingly likely) can trigger a mid-life crisis for a man or a woman or both in a time-is-running-out marriage. Or if the crisis is not successfully resolved, chronic discomfort may be the consequence.

## 5. The Is-This-All-There-Is? Marriage

In the neither-fish-nor-fowl period of your fifties, our society's stereotype is that you are too old to try anything new and too young for Social Security. Frequently in evidence in the Is-this-all-there-is? marriage is an over-the-hill blanket of uncertainty, insecurity, and hopelessness.

## 6. The End-Is-the-Beginning Marriage

Marital life after sixty-five means contending with new, unprecedented aspects of your couple relationship: The loss of one's career identity—what will take its place? How to avoid stepping on each other's toes now that a retired husband and wife are both at home all the time. Contending with the fear of becoming old, ill, and incapacitated. Coming to terms with one's own mortality by choosing either to vegetate in despair or to renew oneself in one's end-is-the-beginning marriage by attempting new achievements in these later years: retiring *to* something instead of retiring *from* work.

## 7. The After-Death Marriage

Because it is very rare for a couple to die together or at the same time, one partner will inevitably become a widow or widower. In the after-death marriage, one typically experiences grief, despair, and self-isolation, continuing to live as if haunted by the dead spouse. Feeling guilt about betraying one's dead spouse if one wants sex or wants to remarry can inhibit self-renewal. One often reimagines one's dead spouse as a saint rather than as a human being with flaws like everyone else. It is important to free oneself from guilt over continuing to live while one's spouse is dead. Constructive engagement with the people and events in this world is the healthiest way to remember a dead spouse.

*Chapter Two*

# A New Marriage of Your Marriage

Michael and Lisa have come to us for help in their relationship, which has turned into a mountain of hurt feelings. They are typical of the many couples we counsel: Michael is thirty-eight, Lisa thirty-six. They are an attractive and intelligent two-career couple who have been married for eight years and think they want a divorce, which is why they came to us. They know we are specialists in divorce, having read one of our previous books, *Creative Divorce*.

Michael has been bitterly angry with Lisa for over a year. "Lisa's changed," he told us. "We agreed when we married that we would never, never have any children, and now I see she's lied to me all that time. Because she's been after me to have a child with her ever since she turned thirty-five. We've had a good life without kids, and I'll be damned if I'll disrupt it. At least I haven't gone back on my word the way she did."

Lisa's blue eyes blazed while Michael talked. She could hardly wait until he finished before she replied, "Since when is smugness a virtue? You're so high and mighty about not going back on your word, but that's just stupidity. Why can't a person change her mind? I was in my twenties when I agreed with you not to have children, because I wanted a carefree life with you alone then. We've had lots of those years, and I don't regret them. But I'm no longer an impressionable girl in my twenties, so now I feel the need for something more. For me, that means having a child. Only women can experience giving birth, and I want that experience before my menopause comes. Why do you have to see this as a threat to our marriage, rather than as an opportunity to make it better? I for one don't like the idea of us thirty years down the road as two old childless crocks playing one round of golf after another or becoming experts in shuffleboard. You're just a self-centered, selfish bastard, not the nice man I thought I married."

Now that they have had their say, they expectantly wait for us to talk about divorce details. However, they are very much surprised when they instead hear us asking them, "Do you really want a divorce, or do you want a new marriage in your marriage, since your old marriage is not working? Perhaps you really want to divorce yourselves from the unskillful behavior that is causing your marital difficulties rather than divorcing each other? Perhaps you are stuck in the wrong marriage (the marriage that came with your marriage license) rather than the marriage that could make both of you happy today?"

It's really not surprising that we would first concentrate on finding out if a couple that is intent on divorcing can turn their marriage around instead. After all, we have both experienced divorce. We both knew that divorce can lead to a happier life (we are now celebrating our nineteenth wedding anniversary!), but the psychological, social, and economic price that must be paid is extremely high.

In fact, it is far easier to improve the quality of one's marriage, providing there is sufficient love left in the relationship, than it is to have what we call a creative divorce. Our own personal experience and work with our clients repeatedly validates this observation. Our own divorce experiences have enhanced our marriage counseling skills; we are very much aware of the many pitfalls that a breakup can cause.

When we asked Michael and Lisa to stop thinking about a legal divorce as their "only" alternative to living together unhappily and think about the possibility of a third way of looking at their marriage (creating a new marriage of their marriage), they later told us it was like a logjam breaking. For, indeed, they still loved each other very much, even though they couldn't stand living together in the hostile way they were now.

With love, new possibilities for happiness opened up in their marriage over the six-month period we counseled with them: They gave up their entrenched belief that they would rather be right than happy. When there is no love left in a relationship, belief in one's own self-righteousness is all that remains. We must be able to forgive ourselves and our partners for the hurtful things done to each other out of lack of awareness.

Michael and Lisa now focused their attention on what would make them happy instead of "right." For starters, this meant stopping the blaming. There was no "good guy" and no "bad guy" in their relationship. On the contrary, they were two well-intentioned people who still loved each other. They were unaware that they were both drilling holes in their marriage boat—in the belief they were trying to solve their problems—and they found themselves sinking instead. For their personal attacks and harsh words simply heightened their anger toward each other. We pointed out that it would be more helpful to them if they would identify their attacking behavior as an "unskillful" way of trying to resolve their difficulties. What they needed to do was to act "skillfully" instead.

The terms *skillful* and *unskillful* are nonjudgmental and direct a couple to focus on identifying behavior that is destroying their happiness and on substituting behavior that will enhance their lives together. These terms are tools that can be used to solve problems rather than wallow in them.

In Lisa and Michael's case, skillful behavior meant talking kindly to each other instead of attacking each other. They could then begin to listen to what each was trying to communicate rather than spending all of their energy defending themselves against each other's harsh, biting, judgmental attacks, attacks that made them forget the issues that had caused their arguments in the first place.

They could now understand that they hated each other's behavior but still loved each other, and that the solution would be to "divorce" themselves from the behavior rather than each other. The first step was to divorce themselves from the foul language they were directing toward each other. To call Michael "a selfish bastard" would hardly persuade him to change his mind. And to say that Lisa was a "liar" who deceived him because she once said she would never want to have a child would prevent Lisa from even considering Michael's point of view.

Divorcing themselves from their blame-making and estrangement from each other was a sign that they were ready for a new marriage of their marriage—the good-enough-parent marriage, to be specific. They had derived great mutual gratification from these childless years, but now that kind of enjoyment was wearing thin. In fact, they were becoming rather bored with each other, as Michael admitted, even before Lisa raised the issue about wanting a child. The need for something more fulfilling in their relationship had arisen for both Michael and Lisa. Lisa was able to quickly recognize that need, which she saw as fulfillment through motherhood, when, at the age of thirty-five, she heard her biological clock ticking loudly. On the other hand, Michael's need for change remained buried beneath his conscious mind.

In counseling with us, Michael became aware that his anger toward Lisa really masked his fear about himself. His anger at Lisa's "betrayal" turned out to be a cover for his very great fear that he might become a "bad" parent, as his own father had been to him. Michael was still bitter about his father's selfishness and rejection of him ("He never came to one, not even one, of my Little League games," Michael told us with tears in his eyes). Once he discovered this about himself, he could acknowledge to Lisa that having a child had also entered his mind, but that the idea that their child would experience the kind of painful life he had had when he was growing up was too horrible to even contemplate. He thought he would make a rotten father, like his dad, and he would hate to subject a child of his own making to misery. Consequently, having a child was out of the question.

Michael's honest expression of these long-buried feelings generated in Lisa a groundswell of empathy for him. Suddenly Michael was no longer a "selfish bastard." Instead, he was a man in pain, conflicted, wanting—yet fearing—to have a child. She could now attend to that pain and say how sorry she was for being so bitter toward him. They were, after all, on the same wavelength: both wanted to have a child, but Lisa welcomed that desire, while Michael fought it. Michael, in turn, apologized for the hurtful things he had said to her. Now they could begin to solve their problem.

As counseling with them progressed, Michael was able to confront his fear of fatherhood and overcome it. Now that his fear had surfaced he could see the absurdity of it. After all, he was not his father, and he did not have to repeat the harm his father had done to him. In fact, he would be a better father than the average parent precisely because he knew what to avoid and what to nourish in a child. This was painfully earned knowledge from his own background. He had far greater motivation than most to make sure his own child would receive from him the kind of parenting he had never had but always wanted.

Much to Lisa's joy, Michael agreed to take the risk of having a child, but he was honest enough to say he was still hesitant and afraid. This was not surprising, because he had lived with this fear of having a child for a long time. That such fear might disappear overnight would be too much to expect, even when it was discovered to be unrealistic.

In our last session together, we pointed out to Michael and Lisa that they had really worked their way through to a new marriage of their marriage. Indeed, this was their third! They had already lived through the movie-marriage-in-their-minds in the first years of their relationship. They then experienced the our-careers-are-everything marriage as they struggled up the career ladder. Now they were ready to experience their third marriage, the good-enough-parent marriage.

In each of these marriages a different aspect of themselves was fulfilled. In their first marriage, there was the fulfillment of enjoying each other, in delighting in the interplay of their personalities; then in their second marriage there was the fulfillment of establishing a sense of competence in the world of work as their careers evolved. Now in their third marriage there would be the fulfillment of creating a family, of experiencing parenthood, which would enable them to broaden their connection with future generations.

We informed them that they would still have to attend to four more marriages throughout their life together! Instead of believing they would be on a permanent plateau once they became parents, they could look forward to these marriages with excitement and anticipation, for they would be fulfilling additional facets of their personalities in these later marriages.

When a couple arrives at what they see as a dead end in their marriage, as Michael and Lisa did, that dead end is frequently a new beginning in disguise—provided there is enough love left in the relationship to allow for mutual forgiveness of the hurt each has inflicted on the other. Michael and Lisa's story is typical of the positive results that can be forthcoming when couples who love each other find themselves at a breaking point in their relationship and are willing to work through their problems in a counseling setting. The "easy road" of divorce turns out to be the "hard road" in the long run.

## Fifteen Guidelines for Creating a New Marriage of Your Marriage in Place of a Divorce

Thousands of couples experience the kind of estrangement that Michael and Lisa experienced before they went to counseling. These couples may have very different reasons for their estrangement than Michael and Lisa's, but if they would ultimately rather be happy than "right," the solution to their problems resides in dealing with their difficulties in a similar way. The guidelines for doing so are as follows:

1. When you are at a dead end in your marriage, seek out a good marriage counselor. It is the strong person who goes to counseling rather than the weak one. If you are too close to a problem to be able to see and cope with it objectively, seeking out a counselor is an affirmation of your desire to do something constructive about your relationship.

2. Realize *you* are not your behavior: you learned whatever self-defeating behaviors you may have long before you married,

many of them as a young person observing your parents and the world at large. Therefore you can unlearn them, no matter how old you are or how long you've been married. Your self-defeating behaviors, not you, will die! This is equally true of your spouse; both of you need to take personal responsibility for making positive, rather than negative, things happen in your marriage.

3. Eliminate judgmental labeling of each other, such as calling each other names, if you have hurt each other. Such labeling attacks the person rather than the behavior (e.g., the person you married is not "rotten," although his or her *behavior* may be "rotten" to you). Name-calling arguments never resolve the issues that give rise to them; they simply escalate your anger toward each other.

4. Consequently, if your marriage has turned sour, rather than believing you have been hurt by a "bad" person, acknowledge that it has soured because both you and your spouse have been unaware of the self-defeating behaviors that led to this situation. When you can begin to see blame-making as simply unskillful behavior, you can focus on substituting nonjudgmental ways of dealing skillfully with the issues that disturb you.

5. Be kinder toward each other. You didn't marry to beat up on your spouse. You will begin to hear each other, to see each other's intent, when you treat each other with at least as much respect as you would a friend or acquaintance. That means not taking for granted the nice things your spouse does, and stopping your hammering away on the "harmful" things you think he or she does. "Thank you" and "I appreciate what you've just done" can go a long way toward defusing potential explosions.

6. Don't mind-read your spouse. If you really had such mind-reading abilities, you would be internationally famous! Always check out what you think your partner might be thinking, rather than telling your spouse what you believe he or she is thinking. In doing so, you will be eliminating the kind of miscommunication that generates marital anger and alienation.

7. Learn to identify the underlying meaning of the unhappy emotions you might be feeling. For example, when you are angry at your spouse, the bottom line is that you are fearful; that is, fearful of his or her not meeting your needs or abandoning you. By focusing on the fear rather than the anger, issues can be resolved rather than perpetuated.

8. Learn to identify and disassociate yourself from the hot flashes of the past, the "I-have-been-here-before" feelings you experience with your spouse. For example, if your spouse scolds you, you may actually feel you are once again a vulnerable little child being chastised by a giant parent. And you may unconsciously react to your spouse as if you are that helpless little child rather than the adult you really are. You can only resolve differences constructively when you and your spouse act as the two adults you are rather than like hurt little kids or stern parents.

9. Distinguish between attachment and concern over the vital matters in your life. To be "attached" to something, like a job or a house or a car, means that your sense of self-esteem, of who you are as a human being, depends on possessing it. A fear-driven life and marriage result from this attitude, for you will always be afraid of losing a possession. On the other hand, though you may still risk losing the things that seem important to you by being "concerned," your self-worth and your spouse's

regard for you won't disappear in the process. *You* are not your job, your house, your car, or any of your other toys. To be "broke" is not the same as being "poor." Material things may come and go, but you will remain a "rich" human being as long as you have the capacity to love and be loved.

10. Determine whether or not you are leading a "prosperous" or a "successful" life. You may be confusing these two concepts and living unhappily in your marriage as a result. For example, when you lead a "prosperous" life, you may focus most of your energy solely on obtaining bigger cars, bigger houses, bigger bank accounts—neglecting your spouse, your family, and your friends in the process. Such an overemphasis on wealth often leads to a bankrupt marriage.

By contrast, a "successful" life is one that balances work, love, and play, so that though attention is paid to earning a living, it is not done at the expense of nurturing your marriage. Practicing a "successful" life enriches you as a human being, something the figures in a bankbook cannot do.

11. Cultivate the art of receptive noticing. Instead of judging your own or your spouse's behavior, notice the behavior instead. Positive change results when you notice behavior rather than condemn it.

12. Practice forgiveness and stop being too hard on yourself and your spouse. Saints are for heaven; there are only fallible human beings on earth. Fresh starts become possible when you forgive each other, and yourself, for the harmful things you might have done, usually out of lack of awareness, in your marriage. Use your guilt over doing such harmful things in a constructive way by understanding why you did those things and how you can prevent them from happening again.

13. Become kind teachers and receptive students to each other. Marriage is an enriching lifetime learning process—a process of becoming a more fully human person with the essential help of one's spouse. This is accomplished by accepting the kind help and insight of your spouse and by applying these same abilities in your spouse's behalf.

14. Cultivate the you-never-know principle. We can carry life's burdens more lightly and with humor when we acknowledge that life is full of surprises, not all of them negative. What may seem like a disaster, such as losing a job, may lead to a better job; a mild heart attack may cause a person to become healthier by motivating a change in diet and exercise; a collision course in a marriage may lead to seeking counseling, leading in turn to a happier marriage. Carry your burdens as feathers rather than two-hundred-pound sacks, for "you never know . . ."

15. Most important of all: Remember that every long-term marriage is really seven marriages of a marriage. If you are feeling bored or taken for granted in your relationship, it might mean you are ready for a new marriage of your marriage instead of a divorce. In place of despair, hope then becomes the exciting new possibility in your life together. The two of you have the power to make that new marriage the reality of your life.

Becoming aware that you will have seven marriages of your marriage changes marriage into a lifetime of self-discovery and the discovery and rediscovery of your partner.

# Part Two

# The Seven Marriages of Your Marriage

*M*arriage is the clue to human life,
but there is no marriage apart from the wheeling sun
and the nodding earth, from the straying of the planets
and the magnificence of the fixed stars.
Is not a man different, utterly different,
at dawn from what he is at sunset?
and a woman too?
and does not the changing harmony
and discord of their variation make
the secret music of life?

—D. H. Lawrence

*E*ach of the following seven chapters deals with a specific marriage of your marriage. The order of these marriages is sequentially typical of the changes couples will experience throughout their lifetime together: The first three (the movie-marriage, the career marriage, and the parent marriage) are typical of the first two decades of marital life; the last four (the time-is-running-out marriage, the is-this-all-there-is? marriage, the end-is-the-beginning marriage, and the after-death marriage) are linked to the later years—as many as forty—of living together. Just as the landscape outside one's home changes over time, so, too, does the couple inside, and the seven marriages are the benchmarks of those changes.

In each new marriage of a marriage, significant revisions of your own and your partner's self-images can take place. When you let go of no longer workable old habits and substitute new behaviors, when you stop taking each other for granted and begin to skillfully identify and adapt to changes, you have an opportunity to improve your marriage. These changes involve transformations as significant as the move from being single to being married and consequently can be identified accurately as the advent of a new marriage of your marriage.

Once you can identify the sequence of predictable developments in your marriage, you can begin to anticipate and cope with them successfully. Marriage need not be an unpredictable jumble of boredom and unpleasant surprises that you feel powerless to cope with and by which you are victimized. A long-term happy marriage requires you and your spouse to recognize and cope skillfully with the "triangles" and "mutual development challenges" in each of the seven marriages of your marriage.

A "triangle" is any person, relationship, preconceived set of ideas, or addiction to things that takes priority over your relationship as husband and wife so that you no longer feel you are the number one person in your spouse's life.

Triangles develop out of lack of awareness, out of drifting unskillfully through one's marriage. You are no longer each other's number one lovers and friends (the most important reason for marrying in the first place). And when triangles are allowed to fester, they create two-can-be-lonelier-than-one feelings of estrangement in a marriage, resulting in a "mini-divorce."

The ability of you and your partner to avoid creating triangles in your marriage, or to deal skillfully with them by identifying and eliminating them when they do arise, is the most essential requirement for maintaining a long-term happy marriage. New triangles can occur as you move into a new marriage of your marriage and leave the previous one behind. The triangles that are specific to each marriage of your marriage—and how you can eliminate them—will be dealt with in detail in the following seven chapters.

Triangles can be seen as poison to a relationship or as mutual development challenges—opportunities to stretch yourselves to solve the specific problems inherent in each marriage of your marriage. You can establish (or reestablish) and maintain a mutual growth relationship in which you can take continuous delight in each other's unique individuality and in your closeness as a loving couple. Mutual development challenges, therefore, are the difficulties married couples experience viewed as the grit that polishes the diamonds of each other's personalities rather than as reasons for anger, alienation, or divorce. They are the means for eliminating the triangles that can poison your marriage.

In contrast to earlier times, couples today marry because each regards the other as the number one person in his or her life —number one as friend, lover, and equal partner. And couples who are already married remain married for the same reason, because it is an essential ingredient for a happy relationship. Consequently, the loss of number one status is the primary reason for the high divorce rate and for marital infidelity.

However, should you feel you are no longer the number one person in your spouse's life, you may be misreading the meaning of that feeling: instead of signalling divorce, it may signify that you are really ready for a new marriage of your marriage. What you may be experiencing is a mini-divorce in your marriage, which can be overcome by resolving your differences constructively instead of breaking up.

The next seven chapters present you with the tools you will need to overcome the triangles and respond skillfully to the mutual development challenges inherent in each of the seven marriages of your marriage. Our analysis is equally applicable to "informal" as well as "formal" marriages. A formal marriage is a legal agreement encompassing first marriages and remarriages. However, informal arrangements, such as living-together arrangements or gay domestic partners' arrangements, are indeed marriages, too, provided they are wholehearted, love-based, monogamous commitments entered into with the desire to make them long-lasting.

As for those never-married men and women who fear the dangerous waters of marriage commitment, we hope what they read here will help them take the plunge, since those waters are more invigorating than they believe.

# Chapter 3

# The Movie-Marriage-in-Your-Mind Marriage

To marry in today's times is to commit an act of courage. The Chinese "curse," "May you live in interesting times!" has become an everyday reality: today is an "interesting" time of unemployment, cynicism, economic insecurity, sexual harassment on the job, rampant crime, worldwide tension, exploitation of the environment, corruption in government, drug and alcohol abuse, child neglect, and emotional, physical, and sexual abuse.

In our society, family life has been so demeaned that millions of people (including those from formerly middle-class families) are condemned to homelessness, one in twelve teenage students has attempted suicide, and the television set is turned on for seven hours a day so that by the time a child is eighteen years old he or she has seen 25,000 TV murders. It is, for people considering marriage, a time when no role models exist who can chart the way to long-term, happy marital life.

So it is indeed an act of courage to marry, but for that very reason it is also the best time to do so. More than ever, in the face of the slings and arrows of daily adversity, we need one special person to love and cherish who is always our trustworthy best friend—one person who will be there for us, reinforcing our courage in times of trouble and eliciting the best from us rather than the worst when we need help. D. H. Lawrence said it best in his poem "Being Alive":

### Being Alive

The only reason for living is being fully alive;
and you can't be fully alive if you are
crushed by secret fear,
and bullied with the threat: Get money, or
eat dirt!—and forced to do a thousand
mean things meaner than your nature,
and forced to clutch on to possessions in
the hope they'll make you feel safe,
and forced to watch everyone that comes
near you, lest they've come to do you down.
Without a bit of common trust in one another,
we can't live.
In the end, we go insane.
It is the penalty of fear and meanness, being
meaner than our natures are.
To be alive, you've got to feel a generous
flow. . . .

The Chinese use the words "interesting times" to mean situations, events, or developments that may be unexpected, disturbing, or upsetting. This is certainly the definition of the times in which we are now living. However, to be "cursed" with this is not necessarily negative. To the contrary—because we all have a tendency to drift through life, seeing ourselves as victims of events over which we have no control, living in an "interesting" time forces us to pay attention to the world around us, to the quality of our lives, to the demands for a better society in which we and our families can flourish rather than waste away.

We stay alert to the fact that attention must be paid to the human condition: we can ignore it only at our personal peril.

In this decade, we are beginning to hear considerable talk about *empowering* ourselves. The word has seeped into the media and everyday talk. That's because a nationwide trend is indeed developing in which people are saying, like the character played by Peter Finch in that old film *Network,* "I'm not going to take it anymore!" They are beginning to rely on themselves to make positive things happen in their lives rather than waiting for plastic politicians or authoritarian gurus to disappoint them again with their deceptions and lies about making the world a better place. This is the self-empowerment you and your partner can begin to practice at the very moment you choose to marry. This chapter is our contribution toward that objective, for self-empowerment begins with arming yourself with new knowledge in place of old, unworkable clichés regarding this first marriage of your marriage.

We call this first of your seven marriages the movie-marriage-in-your-mind. After all, we get more information about how to operate a washing machine than we do about how to function in a marriage; at least a set of instructions and a warranty come with the purchase of a washing machine. But a marriage license comes with no such assurances—all it gives us is a license to fly by the seat of our pants over uncharted waters.

Contrary to popular belief, we may not be the *best*-informed nation in the world. We are perhaps only the *most* informed. This is certainly true about our ideas and conditioning concerning marriage, as indicated in chapter 1. We are flooded with torrents of confusing information about how to create a happy marriage: romantic novels conflict with cynical movies; television sitcoms give you the impression that all marital problems can be solved in half an hour; magazine articles tell you how to "inject" excitement into a dull marriage, as if excitement were just another drug; conflicting psychological "authorities" are quoted in newspaper articles as if they were duelists in sword fights—some arguing for the inevitability of multiple marriages and divorces, others advocating living-together arrangements instead.

It is the rare couple that marries with the realistic expectations and knowledge so urgently needed to make that marriage a success. Think about it. We so often marry in the grip of careless rapture: the challenge of the chase, the "winning" of a desired partner, the fever of sexual excitement, and the amazed delight of finding one's soul mate. Add to these the media images of marriage we internalized as children and the models we inherited from our parents about what it means to live daily in a relationship, and you end up with one movie-marriage in your mind and another in your partner's. This first marriage of your marriage may very well be the only marriage of your marriage if the two of you don't divest yourself of the illusions inherent in each of your movie-marriages. The highest divorce rate occurs in those crucial first three years because all too many couples are unaware of how to divest themselves of their movie-marriages—those lethal combinations of unrealistic and unworkable elements destined to poison any relationship. It is significant that remarriages are as vulnerable to this divorce danger as are first-time marriages; the highest rate of divorces among marriages of any kind occurs within the first three years.

A maximum amount of intelligent effort and understanding is required to overcome the movie-marriage each of you brings to your relationship so that you can progress successfully to the second marriage of your marriage. The two of you must first identify the triangles and challenges that arise in this first marriage and then substitute more skillful behaviors for those that are self-defeating.

# The Typical Marriage Triangles of the Movie-Marriage-in- Your-Mind Marriage

## The I-Never-Knew Triangle

One of the biggest surprises occurs shortly after the honeymoon—that is, the couple's growing awareness of their differences in values, interests, behavior, and beliefs. Of course, these differences always existed, but they were either overlooked, discounted, or thought to be nonexistent during the glamorous, careless-rapture days of courtship. Now, as they settle into married life, the partners find themselves having to attend to the many nonglamorous daily living-together problems that were formerly ignored. The everyday nature of marital life frequently gives rise to disturbing "I-never-knew" feelings about one's partner. In our counseling sessions with recently married couples, these are their most common "I-never-knew" complaints, all resulting from their differing temperaments and upbringing and causing feelings of disillusionment:

She wakes up cheerful every day; he, gloomy . . .

She always sees the best in people; he, the worst . . .

She is disciplined; he, disorganized . . .

She is generous; he, a penny-pincher . . .

She is a worrywart; he ignores problems . . .

She chews over every decision; he makes up his mind instantly . . .

She is talkative; he says little . . .

She is meticulous; he, a slob . . .

She is people-oriented; he, bookish . . .

She is friendly and outgoing; he, shy and withdrawn . . .

She is a day person; he, a night person . . .

She likes long, leisurely breakfasts; he breakfasts on a gulp of coffee . . .

She is forgetful; he always remembers . . .

She is always late; he, always early . . .

She keeps a dust-free house; he couldn't care less . . .

She monopolizes the bathroom; he is a quick splash-in-and-out man . . .

She has a short temper; he slowly burns . . .

She savors extensive foreplay; he wants intercourse first and foreplay later, if at all . . .

She never knew he was so politically conservative, whereas she is so liberal . . .

He lets his clothes bunch up and remain on the floor after he undresses; she always puts hers away in the closet . . .

He never knew she was so fashion crazy; he likes wearing the same suit for days on end . . .

He leaves the toilet seat up; she always has to put it down . . .

She is a bottom-of-the-tube toothpaste squeezer; he always aims for the middle . . .

She tears the toilet tissue from the top; he prefers the underneath position . . .

He never throws away a paper or magazine; she can't stand clutter . . .

She never knew he was a sports-car racing nut; racing bores her to tears . . .

He never knew she wanted a child immediately after marriage; he is unnerved at the very idea of being a father . . .

She never knew he would demand that she always have dinner on the table at six o'clock on the dot as his mother did; she was always flexible about what time to dine . . .

He never knew she disliked his friends as much as he disliked hers . . .

She never knew he couldn't stand her parents' involvement in their lives; she welcomed their concern as a sign of their love for her . . .

He never knew she had so many boring relatives they would have to visit; she always loved large family gatherings . . .

She never knew he was an "I'll-watch-television-and-you-do-the-dishes" man; her brothers always shared household duties . . .

He was an only child and is secretive and self-centered; she came from a large family in which everybody was open and helpful . . .

By the time people with lists like this one seek counseling help from us, their differences have usually expanded beyond the above examples. Their lists have turned into a congealed marriage triangle that has both of them feeling that they really don't know each other—and that frightens them. They each view differences as evidence of flaws in their partner instead of realizing that those traits were always there, they just were not aware of them. Each of them brings to the marriage an entire life history that is necessarily different from their partner's. After all, who would want to share a lifetime with a clone of oneself? How boring that would be!

When the discovery of behavioral differences engenders resentment and hostility, as it commonly does in new marriages, it is important to realize that such resentment is created by one's own attitude. It is simply the failure to understand that such differences are not a sign of withdrawal of your spouse's love for you but part of his or her range of expression. Tolerance and compromise and accommodation come with the territory when you marry, and differences should be viewed as adding salt rather than poison to your relationship. Should the couple fail to accommodate, "I never knew" becomes the "third party" in the marriage. And if the triangle is allowed to fester long enough, it will lead to divorce. In fact, the resentful nurturing of "I never knews" is the primary reason for divorces that occur in the first three years of marriage.

What we have just described about first marriages applies with equal force to people who have been married previously. (Almost 50 percent of all new marriages involve at least one partner who is marrying for the second or even third time.) Their "I never knews" may differ in content, but the same shock of surprise and alienation may take place as a consequence of feeling disillusioned. There are a number of important I-never-knew triangles that remarried couples face that differ from those faced by couples in which neither partner has been previously married. The most important ones are as follows:

### The I-Never-Knew-I-Was-Marrying-a-Crowd-
### in-Addition-to-the-Person-I-Loved Triangle

Gordon is a thirty-nine-year-old man who married Sally a year ago. His complaint is typical of the remarried man or woman who seeks our counsel: "When I married Sally last year, little did I know a baseball team of other people was going to interfere in our lives. There are Sally's teenage son and daughter, who regard me as an enemy; my own three sons, who are pissed off that I married someone else instead of going back to their mother; my new in-laws, who are always telling Sally what to do; and my bitter ex-wife, who is still bad-mouthing me to everyone she meets. And to top it all, Sally's ex hasn't paid child support for the last nine months, so I'm stuck with paying that bill also. My Visa cards are screaming for help!"

In situations like this, priorities can begin to shift, so that more attention and concern are focused on this new crowd of people and problems than on nurturing the love between the new husband and wife. The longer this situation remains unresolved, the greater the erosion of the "number one" feeling between the new husband and wife. The erosion can reach a point of no return.

### The Happily-Ever-After-
### Blended-Family-Illusion Triangle

When a couple with children from previous marriages begins their new marriage, they often believe that their children will no longer feel the anxiety and insecurity that they did while living in a single-parent household. As the thinking goes, all problems with the children will be solved because they will once again be part of a husband-and-wife household, in which they will have positive adult male and female role models they can feel secure about. More often than not, what happens in reality is entirely different: the new, devoutly desired, blended family instead turns out to be an oil-and-water mix. The children may not like their stepparent or feel he or she is a temporary, unwelcome intruder in their lives. Who does the disciplining becomes a big issue. Another is what to do when the kids play their stepparent against their noncustodial parent. (How often have we heard that, during visitation, the noncustodial parent "spoils the children rotten" so that when they come back they demand the same rights at home?) And because the newly married couple love each other, they expect their children to feel the same love toward the new spouse—and are painfully surprised and disappointed when this doesn't happen.

The happily-ever-after-blended-family-illusion triangle can arise from this situation: the feeling that one's partner is the number one person in one's life may be replaced by the alienated feeling that "you love your kids more than you love me." In fact, the inability to skillfully resolve conflicts over stepchildren is the greatest cause for divorce when either husband or wife or both have children from previous marriages.

## The Living-Together-Arrangement Triangle

Many millions of men and women of all ages—from their twenties to their sixties or seventies—choose to live together without actually getting married. This development has escalated in the past ten years since society no longer judges this life-style as negatively as before. Many of these LTA couples do marry, usually within two or three years of establishing a joint household. But a funny thing frequently happens after they take their marriage vows: the compatibility they felt when they were "living together" disappears when they become Mr. and Mrs. The fear of togetherness-strangulation occurs. As one of our clients, Peter, a thirty-four-year-old man who married his live-in partner three months ago, told us, "It's like Halloween every day now that Jill and I are married, like we're scaring each other half to death. You know, neither of us ever married before, and it wasn't like that when we were living together for two years; we felt free then. But now we're like enemies and ready to split up. I don't understand it. Why should a wedding ring make such a difference?"

The answer is, it shouldn't. But it *will* make a difference if you unknowingly bring to your marriage the movie-marriage-in-your-mind that you grew up with. For if that unconscious movie-marriage was a vision of marriage as chronic pain, boredom, and ultimate breakup, you may bring that poison to your marriage and create a self-fulfilling prophecy out of your marital fears. That's exactly what Peter was doing. His parents were alcoholics, and though they never divorced, they instilled in Peter a feeling of bleak insecurity about marriage. His parents were violent, verbally abusive, and always threatening to divorce. When Peter married Jill, he carried that edgy feeling of marriage-as-disaster inside him without being aware he was doing so. Small wonder he was initially hesitant when Jill gave him the ultimatum, "Either we marry, or we break up." But he loved Jill too much to say no. Once they took their marriage vows, however, his fears engulfed him. On the other hand, Jill was hurt and angry; she had expected that marriage would enhance their relationship rather than diminish it. The movie-marriage-in-her-mind had been a good one. Her parents had a loving marriage for over thirty years, until her father died. And although Jill wanted her marriage to be different from her parents', she wanted it to be as successful as theirs was.

It happened they came to us for counseling early enough to prevent their breakup. They were able to come to terms with their movie-marriages and realize that they could create their own positive new marriage in place of hurt feelings and misunderstanding of each other's motives. Peter's fear was based on his unconscious belief that he was still the child-victim who could not influence his parents' marriage for the better, and therefore could not positively influence his own. When he understood that he was no longer that child-victim, he could empower himself to make positive things happen in his own marriage to Jill.

### The Never-Enough-Money Triangle

In the careless-rapture time of courtship, *money* is an unmentionable word. Why stain the purity of a love relationship with such gross terms as *income, spending, savings, budgets, debt management,* and *credit cards?* But freshly married couples soon find out that these terms were written into the marriage license in invisible ink. The discovery that there is never enough money to satisfy all their wants and needs can cause dismay, resentment, fear, and anger early in married life. When a wife feels her partner has let her down by not being the "good provider" she assumed he would be, and a husband believes his wife is not making an effort at getting a better job, the stage is set for losing number one status in each other's eyes.

When two-career couples find their spending exceeding their incomes, mutual accusations of money mismanagement abound. They are in danger of investing so much of their sense of self in their careers that they believe the sizes of their incomes determine their own personal worth. When this happens, each tries to dump the burden of self-inflicted guilt and resentment on the partner, blaming the fix they're in on the partner. When money arguments become a daily habit, the never-enough-money triangle has been created.

This is one of the most lethal triangles in marriage—a triangle that can poison a marriage to death more quickly than any other. That is because the issue of money touches the survival nerve in all human beings. Angry, bitter, hostile words are most likely to emerge in the heat of passionate fear-based arguments, words that cut and sting and may be regretted later. But if such arguments occur too frequently, it may be too late to remedy the harm done to the marriage. Resentments over credit-card living can come to replace your spouse as the number one "person" in your life.

## The Numbers-Game-Sexual-Countdown Triangle

Shortly after marriage a husband and wife may start to misinterpret the meaning of their sex life. Frequently a newly married couple becomes attached to the movie-marriage fantasy that marriage means "happiness ever after" in the form of those marvelous everyday sexual highs they experienced during their careless-rapture courtship days. When those highs diminish in frequency and intensity because of the escalating priorities of struggling to earn a decent living and adjusting to each other's personality quirks, both may feel cheated. They may misread the decline in the number of orgasms and the diminishing frequency of sex as proof that "you don't love me anymore." The more they cling to the idea that fantastic sex is everything in a marriage, the less they cling to each other. When both continue to have a love affair, not with each other, but with their belief that a good marriage means great daily orgasms, neither is number one in the other's eyes anymore. Couples seek confirmation of this belief by falling into the comparison trap. They often check with friends to find out how frequently other couples have intercourse and orgasms and may consider their sex lives dangerously lacking by comparison. However, more often than not their friends will brag (who wants to be judged and found sexually lacking?). Locker-room conversation is notoriously just another version of liar's dice.

Next to the never-enough-money triangle, the numbers-game-sexual-countdown triangle is the one most likely to lead to divorce if not dealt with realistically and skillfully. The insidious seepage of images from television, film, and romantic novels that combine to create the sexual movie-marriage-in-our-minds has affected each and every one of us since birth. Yet without a couple's determined effort to eliminate its harmful impact early in their marriage, they may find themselves divorcing for all the wrong reasons.

## The Mind-Reading Triangle

In the heady days of careless-rapture courtship, when wonderful sex and romantic love take center stage to the exclusion of everything else, couples usually experience a fusion of thoughts and feelings, in which two appear to meld into one. How fortunate to have met the one person in the world who understands your thoughts and feelings!

Not quite! During this premarital stage signals are misread. The focus is on what your partner does for you in that most important but limited arena of romantic love. To be told you are the one special person in your partner's life, that nobody can satisfy him or her emotionally as much as you do, can deflect both of you from the reality that you are two separate persons, each bringing a whole lifetime of prior experience, behavior, thought patterns, and values to your relationship. Consequently, if this isn't understood, the movie-marriage-in-your-mind may generate the false belief that "you must know what I'm thinking even when I don't tell you—or else you don't love me anymore." The mind-reading triangle is based on this attitude.

While writing this, we recalled an absurd but tragic case in which this triangle lasted twenty years and completely eroded a marriage. In this instance, the husband, Arnold, age forty-eight, looked accusingly at his wife, Jane, age forty-five, and said angrily, "You knew when we married that I loved thin pancakes, yet you always made them thick!" Jane was aghast. "Why didn't you tell me that as soon as I made them for you? Now, twenty years later, you tell me! Of course I would have made thin pancakes for you if you had told me you liked them that way. What was I supposed to do? Read your mind?"

For Arnold, the answer to her question was yes. He had lived for twenty years as an injustice collector, accumulating resentments such as this, for he had misread many of his wife's intentions during their marriage. Arnold's mind-reading triangle took over the number one place in their relationship years before the marriage ended.

## The Togetherness Triangle

Where the mind-reading triangle exists, the togetherness triangle is usually not far behind. When a couple becomes attached to the movie-marriage fantasy that they should always agree on everything, any sign of differences between them is regarded as a sign that "he (or she) doesn't love me anymore." As more differences arise between them, each starts to slip from the number one position for the other. Instead of giving up the fantasy of togetherness, they may give up the spouse and keep the fantasy.

This almost happened to a couple, Janice and Ron, who were in their late twenties when they married. Janice's mom and dad always went out together. They never saw separate friends, because they only saw friends that both of them liked. By contrast, Ron's father had always had one weekly night on the town with his male friends, and his mother had had a separate night out with her women friends, so Ron expected the same in his own marriage. He was shocked to discover that Janice thought he no longer loved her when he insisted on spending one evening with his friends. She tenaciously held on to this belief in "togetherness forever," which led to their coming to see us for help. They were alert enough to seek outside help before their hurt feelings created a long-term togetherness triangle, and Janice was able to divest herself of this movie-marriage fantasy. In fact, she now has her own weekly night on the town with her women friends—and thoroughly enjoys it.

## The Best-Face-Forward Triangle

Both husband and wife may be attached to the what-you-see-is-what-you-get movie-marriage fantasy. If, after the wedding, both hang on to the belief that the personality each exhibited toward the other during their courtship is the only one they could continue to like and love, disenchantment may soon set in. Each had put his or her best face forward during the carefree courtship period. But married life is more complex and demanding; other aspects of their personalities emerge. Their courtship personalities were neither false nor deceptive; they were simply aspects that emerged under certain conditions and that will reappear when they experience similar carefree conditions in the future. A couple will inhabit many personalities in their lifetime—economic partners (because marriage indeed is a financial arrangement), career persons, parents, and grandparents, among others. But the couple will continue to feel betrayed if they insist that the only person they can live with is the fun-loving and passionate person they courted. They will feel that they married an imagined perfect person who disappeared after the wedding, rather than the partner who exists in the present.

## The Family-Attachment Triangle

Both husband and wife may be attached to the movie-marriage fantasy that the marital habits of their parents must prevail in their own marriage. He may expect her to keep a super clean, no-dust-on-the-table house because that's the way it was in his parents' home; she may have grown up in a casual household where a certain amount of untidiness was no big deal. His dad may be very reserved in expressing his emotions; she may expect a husband to be a kissing and hugging person because that's the way she saw her dad. She expects him to be a go-getter like her dad; he is more laid back, like his. The more expectations clash about what a good wife or husband must be like, the more diminished each becomes in the other's eyes. Accusations like "Why can't you be a good housekeeper like my mother?" or "Why can't you be as responsible as my father?" start to be hurled like flying plates. Should each partner continue to be attached to the fantasy that Mom and Dad's ways are the only ways to establish a new marriage, each will seem more in love with his or her own parents than with each other.

Charges may begin to fly about that "you love your parents more than you love me" when a husband or wife feels that his or her obligations to their family of origin must take precedence over nurturing their own marriage. A wife may insist that they spend every Friday night with her parents, who insist on this daughterly routine, while her husband finds these Friday nights agonizing bores. Or a mother may give unsolicited advice to her daughter on how to deal with her marital problems, which the daughter dutifully follows even though the advice may be detrimental to the marriage. This inability to set limits on the well-meaning but unhelpful interventions of the parents into their daily lives often materializes into the family-attachment triangle, in which the family is number one and the spouse feels second-best. The longer this situation remains unresolved, the greater the possibility that the marriage will veer toward a breakup.

Because neither you nor your spouse married to get divorced, preventive action is essential to guard against the emergence of any of the triangles we have just discussed or to defuse their potential to destroy your marriage should they arise. For if they do appear and are allowed to go unchecked, a mini-divorce in your marriage can occur. This results from an inability to trust your partner to be the most important person in your life, one who is entirely trustworthy and who always has your best interests at heart. This kind of divorce often manifests itself as a vague but pervasive feeling that "something" is missing in the relationship. A mini-divorce such as this can be the product of an accumulation of triangles as a couple moves from one marriage of their marriage to another. It may not lead to an actual divorce; chronic discontent or boredom can be the consequence as a couple drifts unaware through their lifetime together.

The preventive measures needed to avoid either a mini-divorce or an actual legal divorce are to be found in the mutual development challenges that inhere in each of the seven marriages of your marriage. Each of these marriages has its own unique mutual development challenges.

## Your Mutual Development Challenges

In this first marriage of your marriage there are nine mutual development challenges that will enable you to identify ways to either prevent triangles and mini-divorces from occurring or eliminate triangles that already exist. By following the suggestions outlined below, you should be able to retain or regain your number one status in each other's hearts and minds.

1. **The challenge to define the meaning of the terms *husband* and *wife* in such a way that you can retain your closeness as a loving couple yet remain separate individuals.**

Is your idea of who you are as a husband or wife based on your parents' example? Must your husband be like your father in behavior and attitudes, your wife like your mother? If so, you may feel betrayed whenever your new spouse acts in ways you believe are not "normal." But what is "normal" in your family was more than likely not normal in your spouse's. This challenge requires both of you to share in-depth knowledge of your family backgrounds in order to better understand, modify, tolerate, and accommodate yourselves to the differences between you. Otherwise you may come to regard your partner's differing viewpoints on various issues as attacks against you when no such attack was intended. If, for example, your wife insists on visiting her family on Sunday and you wish the two of you could have a quiet time at home, realize she is not ignoring or imposing on you but may simply be acting out of her family background. Yours may have been quite different. This is not a matter of right or wrong but rather a difference of opinion that needs to be resolved through a shared understanding of your differences. If you react with outrage and indignation, you will only invite retaliation in kind.

In addition, this challenge requires you to define *husband* and *wife* as best friends as well as best lovers, as two people who mutually respect each other because their relationship is based on equality, on shared responsibilities as well as shared delights. Your commitment to such an approach demands action as well as words. Because all human beings are fallible, applying this approach takes practice and persistence. The next time you hear yourself saying or thinking things like "Why can't my spouse be as well organized as my father (or as concerned about housekeeping as my mother)?" stop yourself, for that kind of thinking is a failure to see your partner as the unique individual he or she really is.

2. **The challenge to see your differences in viewpoint as personal attitudes rather than as signs of rejection or loss of love.**

Differences in viewpoint are neither "right" nor "wrong," neither "good" nor "bad"; they are simply products of the different ways you each experienced the world before you met. Your marriage will generate its own seeds of destruction if you persist in maintaining an attitude of "You can only prove you love me by liking only what I like, doing what I do, and thinking what I think."

3. **The challenge to each of you to create an adult relationship with your family of origin so that you can establish an independent life as a couple and still maintain a loving, guilt-free, warm connection with your parents and other relatives.**

The necessity to connect with your parents and with relatives on a new basis is one of the paramount challenges of early married life. You are no longer a child in your family constellation but rather an adult who wishes to establish an independent family life of your own. The act of marriage itself is a breaking away from old childhood family ties and requires the creation of a new adult relationship with your parents. It is an assertion of your right to be treated as an adult capable of making independent decisions and of setting limits on your parents' involvement in your marital concerns.

The degree of parental involvement in your married life will be determined by your answer to the question, Where do my parents' needs leave off and mine begin? Your parents will always be overinvolved in your affairs if you continue to regard yourself as a child in your contact with them. When their desire to be concerned and helpful clashes with your own needs and interests as a couple, it is up to you to set limits.

You may begin to equate loving your parents with the guilty feelings that erupt when you don't abide by their wishes. You will solicit their overinvolvement in your affairs (even if at other times you complain about their "interference" in your marital life) if you run to Mom or Dad with problems and concerns that you and your spouse, not your parents, need to resolve.

The challenge to create a new relationship with your family of origin is ultimately a challenge to relate to your parents as an adult. For example, if your mother or father insists on talking to you on the phone for two hours every Sunday, and you resent having to be home to take these calls because you would be a "bad" son or daughter if you didn't, you are really harming your adult relationship with your parents.

You must be the one to change. The next time they call, have it in mind that you are really harming your adult relationship with them by allowing them this excessive imposition on your own family schedule. In a firm and straightforward way, make an alternative phone visit suggestion that takes into consideration your own family needs. You may have to repeat your new limits more than once, for your parents need to be educated to the fact that they, too, must now deal with you adult to adult. If this challenge is not resolved constructively, your marriage may survive, but it will be beset with resentment, frustration, and anger. For your partner's sense that "your parents always come first, you really don't give a damn about me," may be thought, felt, or voiced with the same intensity in the fifteenth year of your marriage as in the first.

4. **The challenge to differentiate courtship love from married love so that you can develop your capacity to value and appreciate the new and different qualities of married love.**

Courtship love is based on the newness of your relationship: the physical attraction as initially felt across a crowded room and then confirmed when you actually say hello to each other, the sex that is so much better with your lover than with anyone else, the exquisite delight in seeing everything with the same eyes, the desire to be together all the time because you feel that you are dying every moment your lover is not present, the picture of your lover you frame in your mind that haunts your every waking hour and also visits your dreams, the excitement of the chase and the uncertainty of the outcome. (Will he [or she] really be mine forever or be "won" by someone else? I must win this love, because she [or he] has no duplicate on earth, and I could never survive the loss.)

The intensity of these feelings is in direct proportion to the newness of the relationship. You should therefore *expect* that marriage will change the frequency and level of intensity of those highs that made your courtship time so exciting. Marriage requires substantial expenditures of energy on many issues: house or apartment hunting and furnishing, bill payment, job problems, parental involvement and interference, and the need to accommodate to each other's newly discovered personality traits and habits, which are noted with mixed feelings. Small wonder that sexual/sensual highs will wax and wane rather than remain as constant as they once were.

Courtship was the time when you saw only your similarities; in marriage abrasive differences seem to emerge everywhere. If you take this as a sign that the love between you has diminished or died, you have misunderstood what is happening to both of you. Indeed, the "disappointment" you may feel is simply a normal discovery that every newly married couple has to make—the discovery that courtship love, which focuses on intense sexual/sensual gratification and the fusion of two identities, is too fragile a foundation on which to build a lasting marriage. Your disappointment is the bridge to another kind of love—marital love—which can and does provide that solid foundation. Recognize that your new, all-negative view of your partner is as inaccurate as was your previous enraptured courtship view. For example, your husband's silences, which seemed like strength during your courtship but may now seem like weakness, are really neither. They are simply an expression of his personality, and it is up to you to fully understand their origin nonjudgmentally and then work out an appropriate means of accommodation between your needs and his.

Marital love means caring about your partner's welfare and happiness as much as you care about your own. By contrast, in courtship love, two people care about each other only insofar as they can derive instant gratification of their own personal needs. Each of you considers yourself the star performer and your loved one the audience. Marital love requires the ability to put yourself in your partner's place, to understand that the differences that divide you are the differences of two unique personalities, not betrayals of your hopes and dreams. The unconditional willingness of each of you to understand and resolve these differences through sharing your deepest feelings, concerns, attitudes, and ideas is a fundamental component of marital love. Postponing your need for instant gratification, sharing the struggle to triumph over adversities as well as sharing the joys of being together, nurturing each other in crises caused by forces beyond your control and renewing each other's courage in the face of despair, acknowledging the everyday value of your partner with a look or a touch of the hand or by openly appreciating a good meal or spontaneously going to dinner or a movie, trusting your partner to always be there when needed, knowing that he or she always has your best interests at heart even when criticism is given, showing loyalty and dedication to each other in the face of sacrifices that may have to be made—all of these are essential components of marital love that courtship knows little about.

In the context of marital love, the sexual/sensual turn-ons you once had so frequently do not disappear. Instead, they become more like banked fires ready to flame again in appropriate circumstances. And flame they will, more brightly than ever, once they are the product of a life built on a wide range of shared experiences. The closeness has been earned. Sex, then, takes its proper place in your relationship, a place that has been best defined by D. H. Lawrence in *Phoenix,* a book of collected essays:

> For sex, to me, means the whole of the relationship between man and woman . . . that lasts a lifetime, and of which sex-desire is only one vivid, most vivid manifestation. Sex is a changing thing now alive, now quiescent, now fiery, now apparently quite gone. . . . A man says: I don't love my wife any more; I no longer want to sleep with her! But why should he always want to sleep with her? How does he know what other subtle and vital interchange is going on between him and her, making them both whole, in this period when he doesn't want to sleep with her? And she, instead of jibing and saying that all is over and she must find another man and get a divorce—why doesn't she pause, and listen for a new rhythm in her soul, and look for the new movement in the man?

5. **The challenge to never let money problems erode your trust and love for each other.**

Nothing can undermine the quality of your marital relationship more than fear-based squabbles, arguments, and resentments over money. The creation and perpetuation of a never-enough-money triangle is lethal to a marriage and can last a lifetime should you and your spouse fail to come to terms, as early as possible, with how you each regard money issues. Do you insist on controlling the purse strings in your household because you believe that that shows your power to dominate your spouse? Are you using your checkbook as a tool to manipulate your spouse's behavior toward you? Do you panic and feel you will be swallowed up or destroyed if your income is shrinking or if you experience temporary unemployment? Do you believe your status and competency as a human being are primarily defined by the income your job generates? Are you eaten up with envy because others are making more money than you? Do you regard your spouse as a burden, a deadbeat, because his or her income is less than yours or is nonexistent?

If you answer yes to any of these questions, recognize that you are not talking so much about money as you are about yourself. It is a fact of most people's lives that there will never be enough money to satisfy all their wants and needs. Inflation, the possibility of unemployment, unexpected illnesses, children's needs, car and home purchases and repairs, relatives' needs for assistance, limitations on job advancement all combine to make money concerns a normal component of living—now or thirty years from now. To try to improve one's economic position is admirable. But to allow economic concerns to become obsessive, to become issues for argument that make two people who love each other begin to see each other as enemies, is to invite divorce or a lifetime of bitterness. Marital love involves dealing constructively with adversity, not wallowing in it. Seen constructively, economic difficulties are mutual problems that two equals can resolve through budgeting, planning, temporary sacrifices, searching for greater job opportunities, or reordering priorities and values. Essential needs can be separated from the kind of junk-food wants that advertisers create with their seductive commercials. Money problems may continue, but with this approach, the never-enough-money triangle vanishes.

When you realize that the love you have for each other and the trust you have in each other to weather the storms of economic adversity without hostility and resentment are your greatest source of wealth, you can deal with this challenge constructively. These are your real security.

**6. The challenge to become friendly teachers and receptive students to each other.**

As a newly married couple, you and your spouse are potentials in the present rather than finished products frozen into a permanent mold by your previous life experiences. Your marriage is the starting point for your own and your partner's journeys toward becoming adults together. After all, neither you nor your spouse will be the same person five, ten, or fifteen years from now that you are today. What you will become will be determined to a great degree by what you learn from each other during your lifetime together. When you hear people call their spouses "my better half" or "my helpmate," they are intuitively stating that they have learned many positive things from their spouses that have improved the quality of their own lives; their spouses have elicited the best in them.

Any long-term marriage is an adventure in lifetime learning. Every couple that lives together will consciously or subconsciously absorb ideas, attitudes, values, and behaviors from each other and incorporate them into their own sense of themselves. We often hear that couples that have lived together for thirty or forty years markedly resemble each other in the ways they think, speak, and behave, even though they were very different at the time they married. What has happened is that they have learned from each other—learned how to accommodate to each other, learned to resolve problems together, learned to modify their life-styles and value systems jointly, learned to react more appropriately in unison to critical life events. They were friendly teachers to each other without even being aware of it.

By knowing that marriage involves becoming friendly teachers to each other as well as receptive students who have much to learn, your marriage will become more interesting from its inception. If you have a tendency to be dogmatic, your spouse can teach you to become more tolerant. If your spouse acts before thinking, you can teach him or her the value of reflection prior to action. If you are a loner, your partner can teach you to become more gregarious. If your spouse is a worry-wart, you can teach him or her to find more enjoyment in the present. If you are still tied to your parents' apron strings, your spouse can teach you to establish an adult bond with your family. If your spouse is a spendthrift, you can teach him or her prudence. If you are sexually inhibited, your spouse can teach you to enjoy a wider range of sexual excitement.

Failure to respond to this challenge may lead to misinterpretation of your partner's motives, so that every suggestion that is meant to improve your relationship may be misinterpreted as a putdown. You will then turn your spouse into a punitive, rather than friendly, teacher, and you yourself will become the resentful, rather than receptive, student. You can't avoid learning in marriage, but it will be up to each of you either to use your marriage as a basis for improving yourselves as human beings or to sour yourselves on the world.

7. **The challenge to create a caring marital environment that elicits voluntary modification of inappropriate behavior in place of a power-struggle atmosphere in which winning and losing are of paramount importance.**

You and your partner marry in the hope of perpetuating the happiness you experienced in your courtship. Happiness during that time of careless rapture seems to flow from the consequence that your loved one is always "there," always attentive to your bidding, always ready to fulfill your needs. It appears natural that this should be the case, because you are doing the same for your future spouse. But how do you maintain this happiness forever? The answer seems deceptively obvious: such happiness can only be maintained permanently if you insure yourself against the possibility of the "loss" of your loved one. Marriage appears to offer that insurance. A marriage license will "capture forever" the source of your happiness. It will be proof that you have "won" your spouse by triumphing over his or her own reservations about you as well as over any rivals that may also be in the picture now or in the future.

If this has been your attitude toward your loved one, you are not alone, for most newly married couples have also fallen into this trap. And it is a trap—because if this attitude persists after marriage, the happiness that was once "won" will become happiness now "lost." To think in terms of "winning" and "losing" and "capturing" is to think in terms of power. It implies that a good marital relationship consists of exercising control over your partner, dominating and forcing that person to do your bidding and submit to your needs, regardless of his or her feelings. It means seeing every dispute as an issue of right and wrong and of seeing yourself, of course, as always right. Operating on this power principle is the surest way of winning your arguments and losing your marriage.

There is, however, another meaning for the word *power*. When you let go of the belief that the most important issues are who is "right" and who "loses," power can come to mean the capacity to perform effectively.

When you're attacked, the natural tendency is to attack back. But anger is blinding; it is an obstacle to any constructive action, because it gives a false sense of power. Once you reach the point where you can stop yourself from attacking back, you have reached the beginning point of resolving a conflict, for you can then focus on solutions to the problem rather than its perpetuation.

You can then begin to create a caring environment in which it is safe for you to raise issues and resolve them without feeling you will be put down or ignored. The certainty that you and your partner can always share your concerns, including those issues that divide you, can be established only if you see each other as best friends as well as lovers. This means letting go of the conviction that your partner exists solely as an extension of your own needs. You and your spouse must be unconditional equals in your marriage. Neither of you can regard the other as a full-time service industry created for your comfort.

In a caring marital environment, each of you accepts the fact that the needs of your partner may frequently differ from your own, that those needs may, at times, have to take precedence over your own, that sacrifice, responsibility, and obligations come with the territory of marriage. Otherwise, you will forever be surprised and feel ripped off when difficulties arise in your relationship.

Is it really so strange that marriage is beset with difficulties? Whether one is married or not, life itself sets up a series of events that entail economic sacrifices, responsibilities to friends and career, obligations to relatives and society, confrontations with separation, loss, illness, loneliness, and death. A single person is no less immune to these events than a married one.

But to marry is to face these events with a person who loves you and cares about your welfare more than anyone else on earth. The very process of sharing the stresses and strains inherent in adult life can enable both of you to become more fully human, compassionate, and skillful in weathering the storms that time and events hold in store for everyone. But this can only occur in the context of a caring marital environment. Failure to respond to the challenge to create such an environment early in your marriage may result in the kind of relationship in which two feels lonelier than one.

8. **The challenge to expect the unexpected, which comes with being alive.**

President John F. Kennedy once remarked, "Life is unfair," and that was proven by his untimely death. The only guarantee in this life is that we were born and we will die. Everything in between is a product of chance and circumstance and our ability to deal with this fact as best as we can. In marriage, that means not being floored by "surprises," like when both of you said at the beginning of your marriage that you would "never" have children and then ten years later your wife wants to become pregnant. In the context of marriage, "never" does not mean "forever" about any issue. It only means that that is the way you feel in the moment. Adopt the principle that never is not forever, it only feels that way at the time you say it, and you will avoid the injustice-collecting and feelings of betrayal that changes of attitude and circumstances might bring. A parent might suddenly contract a terminal disease; you might experience a miscarriage; you might lose your job; your spouse may have a serious accident; you might find yourself infertile when you wanted a pregnancy—none of these is "predictable," yet they happen all too often. The challenge is to accept that life is unfair (we all die) but to live until we die, not to feel ripped off or singled out for adversities by a malicious universe, but to carry life's surprises like a feather on one's shoulders rather than a two-hundred-pound sack of coal. The fear and bitterness that can result from the feeling that you have been unfairly singled out for tragedy can erode your marriage. When such unexpected things happen—and they will—teamwork can help you transcend your difficulties and affirm that you are still number one for each other.

9. **The challenge to begin to come to terms with the unfinished business in both of your pasts.**

Each of you brings a lifetime of separate experiences to your marriage, and many of these experiences will have a significant impact on your relationship. You and your spouse may not be aware, until well into your marriage, of many of these experiences and how they are affecting your relationship. These experiences often result from a failure to come to terms with childhood traumas.

We frequently counsel couples who have severe sexual problems resulting from the long-buried, often repressed and forgotten fact that, in her childhood years, the wife was sexually abused by her father or a close relative. A year ago, Alan, thirty-three, complained to us in counseling that his wife, Laurie, thirty-one, was always finding excuses not to make love, and when they did she never achieved orgasm. Alan was beginning to think she was falling out of love with him, and they began to argue furiously with each other, which is why they came to us for help. Counseling revealed that Laurie had a basic fear of sexual contact in marriage because she had been incestuously attacked—between the ages of ten and fourteen—by her father. She had not seen her father since her parents divorced when she was fourteen. Laurie had completely suppressed these episodes until she came to counseling.

Her sexual experiences with Alan were fine before they married. It was only after the wedding that they experienced sexual difficulties. Laurie, unconsciously, had linked the idea of being married with her own parents' marriage, in which she was the victim of sexual abuse. Unconsciously, she felt that her marriage would result in sexual abuse to her. She played out this unconscious fantasy with Alan and was able to finally overcome her resistance to sex in marriage by realizing in counseling that she was no longer that victimized little girl. She could let go of her sexual inhibitions once she acknowledged to herself that she had indeed been sexually abused as a child and that she now was a capable grown-up who need never again fear such incest.

This example is unfortunately not exceptional. One out of every four women have experienced some form of childhood sexual abuse. Similarly, millions of men and women are products of alcoholic families. They need to come to terms with how being adult children of alcoholic parents has negatively affected their marriages—not consciously, but out of lack of awareness of this parental legacy.

All people, married or not, have unfinished business from their early upbringing. It can be as poignant as a belief that they were never loved as children, or a feeling of bitterness that they are in the wrong career out of the need to please their parents, or guilt that they hated a parent who physically abused them but has since died.

Whatever your unfinished business, it will have some impact on your marriage. Your awareness of this possibility will go a long way toward eliminating its negative effect. Unfinished business can last a lifetime; however, the sooner you begin to realize its presence, the sooner you can cope constructively with the problems to which it gives rise. Counseling can be of great help in revealing the unconscious pressures on your own personality and on interactions with your spouse that unfinished business creates.

# Chapter Four

# The Our-Careers-Are-Everything Marriage

The second marriage of your marriage usually focuses on concerns in the world of work that crop up once a couple has decided to remain together, even if various issues in the first two or three years of their marriage still remain unresolved. They have learned that they still love each other and have accomplished a degree of compatibility that enables them to move into the our-careers-are-everything marriage.

Today, a majority of couples married less than five years are postponing parenthood until their late twenties or thirties, rather than having children a year or two after marriage as their parents did. It is not necessarily a free choice: In order to live adequately, two jobs are essential. The high cost of living, the fact that almost 50 percent of one's income is required to pay the rent or mortgage, the enormous expenses of pregnancy and birth and afterbirth care, and the uncertainty of maintaining one's job in the face of economic instability all combine to force couples to postpone having children until their incomes and job situations allow for such a major undertaking.

However, the trend toward having children later in life was already under way in the 1980s, when the economy was relatively prosperous. Many couples felt that they needed a greater degree of maturity, a wider range of life experiences, before having children, because that would make them better parents. This attitude, combined with economic necessity, will foster an ongoing tendency for couples to postpone parenthood until their later years, even into their early forties. This can give rise to new triangles unique to this second marriage of your marriage and the need for new mutual development challenges to cope with them.

# *The Typical Marriage Triangles in the Our-Careers-Are-Everything Marriage*

### *The Career-Ladder-Obsession Triangle*

The twenty-four-hour-a-day, seven-day-a-week concern over advancing your career can mean coming home to your spouse at the end of the day only to have a board of directors' meeting about career issues rather than to nurture each other. In the career-ladder-obsession triangle, the person you married becomes secondary to the job you "married."

### *The Later-Not-Now Triangle*

Having a child or taking a vacation together may get postponed repeatedly because of the "demands" of your career. In the later-not-now triangle, saving for a time that never comes becomes the substitute for a shared marital relationship that requires nourishment.

## The Economic-Status Triangle

Equating your self-esteem with the amount of money and the career title you possess, believing that only the man or woman with the most toys "wins," believing that you are loved for your things rather than for who you are places your spouse in a second-best position. In the economic status triangle, your primary energies are directed toward accumulation of material things and career status; your bankbook becomes your love partner.

## The Power-Struggle Triangle

When the spouse who earns more money feels entitled to make the major family decisions, the power-struggle triangle develops, in which concern for maintaining that power position places his or her spouse in an unequal, second-best position.

## The Unemployment Triangle

In uncertain times like the present, the threat of unemployment is ever present in most couples' minds. Angry squabbles over money, overreactions to minor annoyances like tailgating a car, and insensitivity to one's partner's feelings and needs are some of the fear-based actions that can result from the feeling that one's job is at risk. And if an unemployed person believes his or her personal worth or identity is wrapped up in the job, self-esteem may plummet to zero, possibly leading to psychological depression and temporary sexual impotency. These are the components of the unemployment triangle: the number one party in your life is no longer your spouse but your fear.

## The Old-Money Triangle

If there is a never-enough-money triangle for most couples, for some there is a too-much-money triangle based on "old money." Old money is inherited wealth that was created generations ago. The inheritance is usually in the form of a sizable trust fund that enables the recipient to lead a life of pure self-indulgence. This is not necessarily a blessing. Because the money was not earned, there is ever present the uneasy feeling that whispers, "Am I loved for who I am, or for my money?" A person with a trust fund may feel a lack of self-esteem similar to that of an unemployed person of limited means. Unless motivated to put effort into attaining a career that will furnish a sense of personal accomplishment, he or she might drift through life without ever really believing that love, rather than money, is at the root of the marriage. The old-money triangle creates a situation in which the monied partner distances his or her spouse from the number one position out of the fear that it is the money that he or she is after.

## The Job-Unhappiness Triangle

In many instances, a husband or wife or both feel "trapped" in the jobs they have. They work out of necessity, and if pressed for an honest answer will admit they don't like the jobs they have but see no possibility of getting better ones.

This is particularly true of women, who, though they now constitute almost 50 percent of the work force, are victims of "the glass ceiling." They are prevented from achieving high career status and tend to be in the dullest, lowest-paying jobs. Indeed, 80 percent of all clerical and service industry workers are women. Women also earn only 70 percent of what men earn for comparable work, which compounds their feeling of job discontent.

If the source of such unhappiness is not understood and discussed with one's spouse, this discontent can spill over into the marriage. A wife may unconsciously distance herself from her husband, feeling that all men, including her husband, are enemies who hurt women. The number one focus shifts from her husband to feelings of depression or unhappiness.

Because men have been programmed by our society to believe that their value and worth depend primarily on their career status and income level, a husband who is unhappy with his dead-end job and small paycheck can feel he is unlovable. If he doesn't express these feelings to his wife, he may feel rejected, even when his wife still considers him the number one person in her life. He becomes the victim of his own self-created job-unhappiness triangle, because he will act out an "I wouldn't want to belong to any club that would have me as its member" attitude toward his wife, thus rejecting her before she can reject him.

## The Sexual-Harassment Triangle

Every working woman knows, either consciously or subconsciously, that some degree of sexual harassment is a fact of the business world. We have often been told by our women clients (whether they are lawyers or doctors or students or teachers or clerks or secretaries) about the indignities they have endured in their jobs solely because they were women.

Sexual harassment means more than demands for sexual favors. It also means being bullied, demeaned, and kept at low-level positions without any hope of advancement solely on the basis of gender. To be discriminated against solely because of one's sex is a gross attack on one's self-esteem: "When my supervisor told me I'd have to go to bed with him or lose my job, I felt I'd been raped," Janice, an assembly line worker, told us. "In medical school, I was always called 'girl' by the teaching doctors. I felt I was a second-class citizen. It was as though the women's movement's demand for fair and equal workplace treatment had never been heard of by any of those pompous asses," said Laura, a recent medical school graduate. "Every time I ask for a higher-rated job in my division, I get told none is available. But I notice all those jobs are filled by men, and the last time a job opening occurred, you bet another man was chosen to fill it," said Mary, a computer operator who had studied to become a computer programmer but was never given the opportunity to demonstrate her skill.

Touching someone's body without her permission, telling lewd jokes, making suggestive comments, discussing porno movies—all usually pass without complaint, because they are done by men who have the power to fire women or punish them by changing their jobs. If the women complain to a supervisor, their complaint is laughed at or ignored.

We hear some of our women clients rationalize sexual harassment by denying its very existence: "Oh that's the way men are, they don't mean anything bad by it." Of course, it's "bad," if only because such intimidation trains women to remain second-class, victimized citizens. Other women who experience sexual harassment as "rape" usually feel so intimidated by their own feelings of powerlessness to correct this behavior, by their fear of losing their jobs, that they internalize their anger, which becomes a form of depression, and translate their feelings into low self-esteem.

This sense of victimization and powerlessness turns into the sexual-harassment triangle if it persists long enough. One's spouse's status as number one vanishes in the swamp of feeling demeaned and powerless on the job. That feeling can so easily spill over into one's home life: it's safer to kick your spouse at home than to kick the boss on the job.

### The Hostile-Work-Environment Triangle

A hostile work environment has nothing to do with sexual harassment as such. It has everything to do with power relationships in the business world—relationships that affect both sexes.

A hostile work environment is an environment in which employees of both sexes are demeaned, victimized, and trained to be helpless pawns in a game run by people who have the power to determine whether or not an employee will be "permitted" to continue to hold a job. It is sometimes a hypocritical environment in which a giant corporation will call itself and its employees "a family."

We have heard many stories from our clients who learned the hard way what the term *family* can mean in this corporate sense. "I put in twelve years with the firm, believing it was what they said it was, a family," Arthur, a thirty-nine-year-old man, told us. "And then I was fired, just like that. Would you believe it, one week before Christmas without any notice whatsoever! I thought the company would take care of me. Isn't that what a 'family' is supposed to do? Like hell! . . . I don't know if anyone will hire me now that I'm turning forty. I'm lucky I have a supportive wife who says she will always love me, job or no job. Otherwise I feel my life wouldn't be worth living."

The feeling that we must take whatever is dished out by our employers, who pull rank on us rather than treating us as the thinking and feeling human beings we are, that we are the victims of shell games our politicians play on us, that we are forever vulnerable to advertising agencies and television commercials that tell us to buy things we don't need—these feelings have become universal in our society. The surges of frustration and anger that a partner may experience, whether hidden or overt, at this daily assault on his or her self-esteem can create a sense of isolation, cynicism, loneliness, and estrangement in oneself that can erode the love relationship. When that happens, the hostile-work-environment triangle has superseded one's spouse as the number one "person" in the marriage.

## Your Mutual Development Challenges

These are mutual development challenges that confront you and your spouse when you find yourselves living in the our-careers-are-everything marriage:

1. **The challenge to resolve your career and economic dilemmas in ways that will move you closer together as a loving couple, because the tendency in this marriage is for each of you to turn your spouse into a roommate rather than a lover.**

Your answers to the following questions can clue you in to whether or not you are responding constructively to this challenge:

Do you really listen and care about what has happened to your spouse on the job?

Does only one of you ask or tell the other?

Do you refuse to share your concerns about your job because you think your spouse wouldn't understand the problems you are facing at work?

Are you too embarrassed to tell your spouse that your boss reprimanded you or that you are terrified about making a presentation at a company meeting?

Do you try to put yourself in your spouse's shoes and understand that what might be no problem to you might be a great problem to your partner, requiring your helpful feedback?

Do you admire your spouse's strengths on the job as you would a colleague's, or are you secretly envious that he or she possesses these qualities?

Do you feel you are entitled to a greater say in family economic decisions and in household management because you are earning more money than your spouse?

The degree to which you share your vulnerabilities as well as your strengths, your empathetic understanding of your partner, and your willingness to care as much about your partner's welfare as you do about your own will determine whether or not you have avoided setting up a competitive husband-wife relationship in which power and domination based on self-centeredness define the quality of your lives together. Should you bring the competitive atmosphere of office life into your household, your marriage will become little more than just another part of your business world, rather than a sanctuary from it.

## 2. The challenge to redefine your own personal identity.

Do you primarily think of yourself as a wage earner or career-pursuer, with everything else secondary? If so, where does being a loving spouse, a caring son or daughter or friend, or a socially responsible person fit into your sense of self?

There must be a fine line between bringing home too many small problems and details from the office and sharing critical concerns about your workday that really need empathetic feedback from your spouse if you are to resolve them. It is also possible to share your workdays with each other unskillfully to the extent that every night at home can become a rehashing of the day's business instead of a marriage. When this happens, you need to add balance to your lives together. Both of you are more than just career persons. You have other pressing emotional needs to fill. When you find yourself complaining crankily that you "must" spend evenings and weekends working or thinking about work in order to advance yourself, it is time to go out and have some fun with your spouse. When you find yourself seeing after work only those people who can be of use to you in a business way, it is time to catch up on your friendships and your relationships with your spouse, parents, and relatives. If you hear yourself complaining that you are forced to spend all your "free" time socializing with business people who bore you and your spouse, recognize that you are creating your own jail. Restoring pleasurable company of your own choosing to your life as a couple will, in the long run, enhance your outlook on your job as well as your marriage.

3. **The challenge to make gender equality in your two-career marriage a reality in deeds as well as in words.**

Few people today would dare voice the absurd opinion that women should remain in a subservient position because they are less able and intelligent than men, that they are born nurturers and little else. Such nonsense no longer dominates. However, old, sexist family and societal programming can often defeat a husband's best intentions to practice gender equality and true partnership in his marriage. At the unconscious level, significant traces of such male chauvinism may exist in husbands who intellectually are honestly committed to an equal partnership; their programming from their early years regarding what a "real" male is supposed to be unconsciously undermines such a commitment in practice. If you are a husband in a two-career marriage, your honest answers to the following questions can help you determine whether this gap exists within you:

Do you really like the fact that your wife works?

Do you take pride in your wife's professional competency for her sake as well as your own?

Would you secretly like it better if your wife greeted you at home every evening with a clean house, refreshments, and a hot dinner, even though she has worked as hard as you and put in as many hours in her own job?

Do you really do your full share of the housework without continual prodding from your wife or without feeling argumentative and resentful because you feel you are always getting the short end of the stick?

Do you view going with your wife to entertain her clients as being as important as her helping you to entertain yours?

How would you feel if your wife made more money than you? If she is already making more money, do you have mixed feelings about that fact? Do you talk to her about your feelings?

Should you see traces of your upbringing staring at you in your answers to these questions, there is no need to flagellate yourself. You are neither a hypocrite nor a dissembler, but simply a person who has been unaware of the extent to which your own upbringing still dominates your behavior toward your wife.

We live in a time of transition, when married couples are free to pursue ways of relating to each other that are consistent with the reality that they are equal partners. These are the men and women who must create the role models for a good two-career marriage, because the models that used to exist are no longer applicable. And because they are pioneers, they will invariably make mistakes and fail and fall prey to unrealistic expectations, pain, disappointment, and discouragement. To expect otherwise is to invite anxiety and depression in the pursuit of a nonexistent ideal marriage. There are many young, idealistic couples whose marriages end in bitter disappointment at the end of a few years when they find out that putting their belief in equality into practice in their relationship differs substantially from making an intellectual commitment to equality.

Here's a typical scenario: a husband comes home after work and automatically sits in the living room with a bottle of beer by his side and a newspaper in his hands. Where's his wife? In the kitchen making dinner, of course. The young man is acting just as his father did in his marriage. This happens even when the wife has put in a full day's work at the office as well. Both of them revert unconsciously to the sexist roles they were conditioned into despite their intellectual renunciation of such roles.

Because the present generation of young married couples lived most of their lives in their parents' homes, where they were exposed to traditional conditioning, should it be so surprising that they tend to revert to old-style behavior when they marry? Many couples are so shocked at this reversion that they start accusing each other of being liars and deceivers who never meant what they said about their commitment to equality in their relationship. The key to meeting this challenge is for both husband and wife to acknowledge the power of their upbringing to interfere with their present best intentions. Instead of bitterly criticizing each other, they should perhaps be self-critical for being so hopelessly naive as to believe that brave words (like *sexual equality*) can be realized simply by being uttered.

When you become nonjudgmentally aware of the extent to which you are affected by family conditioning, you can take steps to bridge the gap between your words and deeds by sharing with your spouse your realization that this gap exists and by noticing the times you find your old attitudes and behaviors coming into play in your relationship. When you notice them, you then have the power within you to eliminate their presence in your marriage.

It is true that women have been demeaned by men as a consequence of the cultural climate in which men grew up, and that significant traces of this early conditioning exist in the present-day behavior of well-intentioned men. But it is equally true that many career women who firmly believe that they are (at least) men's equals in intelligence, ability, and competence also exhibit residues of these same conditioned, sexist attitudes. For when these women were growing up, they, too, were taught by society and by their own mothers to be unassertive, to believe that their husbands' careers came first and that nurturing was the most important and desirable quality in a woman. In essence, women themselves were taught to believe that men, by nature, come first in society.

If you are a wife with a career, you can determine the extent to which your own past programming might be eroding the quality of your relationship with your husband by answering the following questions:

Do you feel you are in competition with your husband regarding who has the best job and who makes the most money?

If you are, is the feeling one of healthy competitiveness as in a track race, or a feeling of guilt or anger because you are competing with him?

Do you do more than your fair share of the housework rather than hold your husband to his end of the bargain because you don't want to make waves?

If your husband is making more money than you are, do you feel guilty when you spend money on yourself because you believe you are spending "his" money?

Do you allow your husband's purchasing desires to take priority over yours because he makes more money than you do?

Is he "more equal" than you are in deciding on big-ticket purchases like home electronics, cars, houses?

Do you feel you are entitled to less decision-making power in your household because your husband makes more money than you do?

Do you label the total income you and your husband make "our" joint income, or do you regard the earnings of each of you separately as a measure of the power each of you brings to your marriage?

How would you feel if you made more money than your husband? If you are making more money than your husband now, do you feel guilty or secretive about sharing that fact with friends?

Do you consider your husband's job a "safety net"? How would you feel without it?

Your answers to these questions will provide you with evidence of the extent to which your feelings are still based on early life conditioning and are in conflict with your intellectual belief that you are entitled to full equality in your marriage. If you discover that substantial residue of your past conditioning continues to shape your present behavior, you may very well be giving double messages and conflicting signals to yourself and your husband. You may be excessively dependent on your husband while believing you are a truly independent person. And you may be acting on an old, programmed belief that when major decisions are involved, your husband's desires come first, while at the same time insisting on your right to be considered an equal partner.

You can come to terms with these residues of your past in the ways discussed above by becoming aware of them and then noting and discussing them with your partner when they come up. Otherwise the primary enemy of gender equality and true partnership in your marriage may very well prove to be you.

4. **The challenge to two-career couples to serve as positive role models for a generation faced with seeking answers to the unprecedented problems created by this new kind of marital option.**

For the first time in history, two-career marriages, in which wives have freely chosen to make establishment of their careers their top priority, are now commonplace in American life. For such couples, children often become a second priority, to be planned for when the couple reaches their late twenties or early thirties. If you and your spouse are such a couple, you will find no ready answers for how to maximize enjoyment of marriage and career as you try to cope effectively with the problems and complexities inherent in this arrangement. You have no guidelines and no answers to go by, because you are living in a type of relationship for which there are no precedents. Should you postpone having children or opt for a childless marriage? Should your career requirements take precedence over your marital and family needs? Should you demand everything—a good job, children, a warm family life—and insist that everything materialize at once? Should you expect to resume your career once you take a leave of absence to have children? There is as yet no Dr. Spock to answer questions of this nature. You and your spouse, as well as all the other two-career couples, have been given the power to shape that history. The answers you two agree upon will be the models for the future. For better or worse, you will become role models whose behavior will influence future generations.

Should you fail to develop appropriate solutions to the challenges outlined in this chapter, you could prove to be negative models. Divorce from a chronically unfulfilling marriage could well be the consequence of ignoring the triangles and challenges that await you in your two-career marriage, and that is not a legacy anyone would wish to leave for future couples contemplating a two-career marriage.

On the other hand, you have the opportunity to be explorers in a profound new life adventure—the adventure of innovating, through trial and error, a creative marital arrangement that can validate for others the two-career marriage and its capacity to offer both great happiness and the opportunity to fulfill the widest range of your potential. The choices will be up to you. Couples in the midst of making these choices often complain that they can't have it all. But the fact is, you can have most of it, perhaps not all at once, but over a lifetime, and that's a great achievement. Learning to accommodate to realistic limitations is also part of successful living.

5. **The challenge to recognize that fear is behind marital anger, and that in order to eliminate the anger, you first have to identify and eliminate the fear that gave rise to it.**

When we marry we open ourselves up to becoming fearful —fearful in the way we felt as children whenever we thought we would be abandoned by our parents. We hear many stories from our clients about how that fear of being abandoned by their parents, emotionally or physically or both, created reactions of terror and anger. John, for example, regularly heard his mother and father scream at each other, threatening to divorce. Scary visions of being nine years old and left alone to fend for himself would attack him. Although his parents never divorced, the constant threat of it hung over John's head like a sword ready to destroy him. His fear of abandonment turned into smoldering anger at his parents for causing him pain. He "got even" with them by becoming unmanageable: refusing to go to bed on time, cutting classes, indulging in alcohol and marijuana in his early teens—all acts of aggression and anger designed to retaliate against his parents since he thought they were threatening to abandon him by divorcing each other. Nothing is as frightening to children as believing that they will be abandoned by the people they depend on for their very survival.

A household in which the mother or father (or both) is an alcoholic creates abandonment feelings of terrifying intensity. A parent might promise, while drunk, to take the child to a party or the zoo and forget the promise and disappoint the child. An angry child—angry at the parents' abandonment of the promise—is the result of that betrayal. Or a parent will disappear on a three-day alcoholic binge; the child then experiences the terror of physical and emotional abandonment. It is no accident that adult children of alcoholics are quick to anger; it is a consequence of such acts of abandonment in childhood.

Therefore, it is not surprising that the fear beneath marital anger is fear of being abandoned, either emotionally or physically, by your spouse—the most important person in your life, the one you feel connected to in a family way. It's an "I have been there before" feeling of the kind one only experiences as a child within one's family of origin.

Because anger is a major trigger of marital breakups, it is extremely important to diffuse its impact by uncovering the fear that gives rise to it. In one form or another, it is the fear of being abandoned by the person you love the most.

Directing anger against a loved one is like scratching a mosquito bite. It may feel good while you are doing it, but when you stop you are the worse for the scratching: you have risked infection or pain, and the itch remains or becomes more virulent.

Instead of resolving a problem that might have ticked you off at your partner, exploding with anger simply perpetuates the problem. The person against whom the anger is directed experiences it as a personal attack rather than as an attempt to deal with the issue that has given rise to the anger. And instead of responding to the issue, the person attacked will counterattack as a means of defending his or her sense of self, which the anger attack has undermined. Anger also increases the adrenaline flow, giving one a false sense of power, a sense that one is in control of the argument rather than fueling its fire. When anger takes center stage in your relationship, both of you can get sucked into justifying your anger with thoughts of "I'd rather be right than happy." Every unresolved angry confrontation with your spouse becomes another step toward demoting your spouse from the number one position in your life. If your spouse is angry, try to understand the fear that is below the surface.

Angry confrontations tend to be frequent in the "Our-careers-are-everything" marriage, because nothing will give rise to fear-based arguments as easily as issues of career competition, unhappiness in the job, sexual harassment in the office, a totalitarian work environment, or the threat or reality of unemployment. When you find yourself picking a fight with your spouse and getting angry, ask yourself, "Why am I so fearful?" rather than saying, "My spouse is making me angry." You will find the anger diminishing when you get to its root cause, which is usually a fear of abandonment that stems from low self-esteem. It's as if you feel you wouldn't be loved if your spouse really knew how worthless and helpless you think you are. For example, should you become unemployed through no fault of your own, recognize that the source of your anger is the fear that you will be thought less of (that is, be emotionally abandoned) by your spouse instead of picking fights with her or him over minor issues that mask your anxiety over the job loss ("Damn it, why can't you ever keep this place clean!"). In the process of sharing your fear with your spouse, you will discover that your anger will vanish and that both of you will begin to deal with this problem constructively. You will experience your partner's support and encouragement—the qualities of a loving spouse.

Similarly, instead of hiding your feelings of unhappiness about your job and starting angry arguments over trivialities ("Can't you ever stop talking to your friends on the phone? I'd like to use it too, but you hog it all the time!"), recognize that your anger could be a cover for your fear that your spouse finds other people more interesting than you, which is fear of being emotionally abandoned. Once you make this connection, you can share your fear with your spouse and, in place of anger, have a positive discussion about alternative job possibilities.

For example, this happened recently to Jack, forty-one, and his wife, Ellen, thirty-nine, who had been having fights over minor issues like, "Jack, why do you always leave the bathroom door open when I've told you a thousand times to close it when you've finished?" Their real fear was over the fact that the medium-size department store where Jack had been personnel director had gone bankrupt, and he hadn't been able to find a new job. Once they worked through their anger and fear in counseling sessions with us, they began to see new hope. Jack had been in personnel work for nineteen years and found that he was sick and tired of it and had wished for years that he could change careers. "The pay was so good that I didn't want to scare Ellen by saying I'd like to get into another line of work."

It was as though I had golden handcuffs on me. And besides, here I was, just turning forty, so where was I to go?"

Ellen was completely surprised that he had kept this secret from her. It turned out he didn't tell her because he didn't want to worry her. She, however, told him she was more worried that he had kept it a secret. "I knew you looked distant and worried, and I thought maybe there was another woman, and that made me very anxious and touchy. I'm glad you finally told me here what was really going on inside you. Maybe losing the job is the best thing that ever happened, rather than the worst."

And that turned out to be exactly right. The "you-never-know" principle that we discussed in an earlier chapter worked for them. Indeed, Jack's job loss lead to his obtaining a better one, one that he very much enjoyed, in an entirely new field. As they started to share ideas about "What next?" Jack stated that he would like a job in one of the helping professions. "There is no satisfaction in working for companies that are only interested in making a buck at their employees' expense. That is all I've been doing all my life. I'd like to get into something that makes a worthwhile contribution to society instead, but I'm forty-one, and isn't that too old to start over?"

No, forty-one wasn't too old to "start over." First of all, he wasn't starting from scratch; he had almost twenty years of experience in the business world and had accumulated many skills that could be transferred to careers other than personnel, and where his age could be an advantage instead of a hindrance. For example, he enjoyed working with people and helping and guiding them, which was part of his job as a personnel director, and he was very good at these tasks. Those were necessary, in fact absolutely required, skills in many jobs in the helping professions. In addition, the helping professions needed mature counselors who had experience working with people: being forty-one would be an asset. And, most important of all, in this time of layoffs and recession, jobs opportunities in the helping professions, particularly those dealing with people with drug and alcohol addictions, were expanding rather than disappearing. As Jack and Ellen became aware of these facts, Jack took a short-term training program about counseling adult children of alcoholics. As an adult child of alcoholic parents himself, with his empathy and understanding of the particular problems they faced, he was more valuable to the profession than many others looking for this kind of work. The fact that he could counsel people individually and in groups (which he had been doing in personnel work for many years) made him the perfect choice for the hospital that hired him.

The adversity of unemployment drew Jack and Ellen closer together. You never know when a crisis can turn into an opportunity—until you make it happen.

When a husband and wife love and care for each other, the sharing of fears and vulnerabilities is welcomed rather than rejected. After all, isn't having a best friend, who you can trust to help you reinforce your courage and overcome your personal unhappiness, one of the reasons for marriage? Is it any different with remarried couples or living-together couples or gay and lesbian domestic partners? The question answers itself. The specific issues causing angry confrontations may differ for each of these marriage variations, but the essential reality is that fear is behind the anger, just as it is with first-time married couples. Whenever two adults of whatever sex are involved in a totally monogamous love commitment, intense feelings of anger against a partner can be traced to the root fear of being emotionally or physically abandoned. Abrasions and confrontations are inevitable in any committed relationship, because they arise out of the very act of sharing one's life with someone else. When the anger is dealt with skillfully by connecting with the fear that activates it, constructive resolutions of the issues that divide a couple become possible. A "we would rather be happy than right" feeling can then prevail and nurture the relationship.

6. **The challenge to *(a)* recognize that the national publicity and debate over such issues as sexual harassment on the job are expressions of the continuing relationship revolution in our society and *(b)* utilize that reality to improve your marriage.**

We mentioned previously that we are in the midst of a relationship revolution. It emerged in the mid-sixties and is an ongoing process that is continuing today and will continue for a long time to come. The fact that sexual harassment of women employees has become an issue of national attention and concern is indeed a "revolutionary" event, in the sense that it is another expression of women's demand for nothing less than authentic equality with men. The dictionary defines *revolution* as "an activity or movement designed to effect fundamental changes in the socioeconomic situation," and that is what the drive for full equality between the sexes is all about. In fact, the *women's revolution* has become so accepted a term that magazines such as *Vogue* can write approvingly of "the revolution that put women in the workplace," as it did in its September 1991 issue. However, putting women in the workplace was only the first step in the drive toward complete equality of opportunity and professional respect. If full equality is to be realized, sexual harassment on the job must be completely eradicated. Such harassment is really an attempt by men to "keep women in their place," a way of exercising power to dominate women and reinforce the old stereotype that women in or out of the work force are still the lesser sex.

Out of the national debate over sexual harassment can emerge a greater understanding, a mutual recognition of women and men as equal partners rather than antagonists. A constructive revolution involves an often wrenching revision of values, expectations, and behavior. The uproar between the sexes should be welcomed as an opportunity to improve relationships rather than destroy them.

In our marriage, we share a personal commitment to gender equality, and our counseling work is directed toward helping our clients attain that kind of equality in theirs. It is our belief that no marriage, or any other kind of committed relationship, can achieve long-term happiness unless true equality is practiced. We emphasize "practiced" because it has become trendy for couples to claim belief in such equality; it's the socially acceptable thing to do. However, when women work as hard and long as their partners all day and then come home and perform most of the housework, that's hypocrisy, not equality.

Because the issue of sexual equality has the most profound effect on marriages today, a more empathic understanding of what men and women are really like is absolutely essential. We attempt to help our clients toward such empathic understanding by sharing some of our own personal background and why we believe equality is not a choice but an essential component of any good marriage. Here is Mel's story, and then Pat will share hers.


### Mel's Story


Pat and I have often organized Learning to Love Again groups for men and women who have experienced broken relationships. At the end of the last of ten sessions, we ask the men and women who have taken the course (usually there are an equal number of men and women) what they have learned the most from it. There are always at least one or two women who will say, with considerable surprise in their voices, "Until I took this course, I never knew that men had feelings!"

There is always a look of hurt confusion on the men's faces when they hear this, because if there is one thing they know about themselves, it is that they hurt and bleed and feel all the emotions that women feel; they just express them differently, usually hiding them from public view.

When we hear such statements from women, Pat and I often comment that it seems as if men and women in our society arrived here from two different planets. And they communicate as if they were two ships blindly passing each other in the night.

I have great empathy for those men in our groups, because I, too, experienced their hurt confusion at the time of my own divorce in the 1970s. I have written about this in *Creative Divorce*. When I divorced, I had two teenage daughters but was very unaware about how women felt. All I knew then was that my marriage hadn't worked. But I was determined to find out what I had done—out of unawareness rather than malicious intent—to destroy the marriage.

I had grown up, the eldest of three children, in a household in which the old stereotype of father as sole wage earner and mother as homemaker prevailed. As the oldest son I had privileges of which I was then unaware: I didn't have to do a damned thing to help around the house, not even take the dishes off the table after meals. Mom did everything, and I assumed that was the way God made the world. The message I believed God sent out to men all over the world was that women were the lesser, the second sex. Obviously men were more important, because we were the wage earners without whom food, shelter, and education would disappear.

I was also programmed to behave in ways sanctioned by our culture:

Helping women at household tasks like washing dishes would make me feminine.

Never cry, because only women cry. Don't ever admit you

wanted to cry when your mother or father died, for that wasn't manly (I bled internally but showed no tears the day my own father died).

Never admit to your wife that you are scared or anxious about your job when layoffs are rumored.

Never ask for help at a gas station if you lose your sense of direction when you are out driving with your wife, because that would demonstrate your lack of knowledge. Men should know everything even when they don't.

Men need sex more than women, so it is a man's right to demand sex, and women should always accede to that demand. (How absurd that seems today!)

Always say, "I'm fine," when your wife asks you how your day was, even when you are falling apart inside.

Never admit you are ill or need a checkup. Men are always strong and in control.

Men are always entitled to make the big decisions unilaterally, like buying a car. It's all right, however, to allow your wife to choose the color.

Share with your wife all the achievements of your day, but never the hurts and disappointments, because she would think less of you if you told her you were vulnerable.

What I have just enumerated are nine pathways to a divorce rather than a happy marriage. Practicing the behavior that the culture of the 1950s prescribed for men as ways to win the approval of their mates led to estrangement rather than closeness. Implicit in such male ways of relating is the assumption that women must cater to men's needs, but men can ignore women's. Women of that time felt demeaned but believed they had no alternative but to stuff their anger; they were powerless, their economic security depending on the male. That anger turned inward exhibited itself as depression, as "the problem that had no name," as Betty Friedan called it in her revolutionary book *The Feminine Mystique.*

In the 1970s, when women began to feel that they were not the lesser, the second, sex and started to insist that they be treated equally at home and have equal work opportunities, we experienced the divorce explosion. I was a statistic of that explosion.

The traumatic effect of my divorce after a long-term marriage forced me to reevaluate my own sense of self as a human being rather than as a male stereotype. I had come into my first marriage with the best intentions in the world. We men have a fund of goodwill toward women, but we were never given the tools with which to relate to our spouses in a way that they had every right to be treated—as equal partners. It is a fact that every poll taken from the 1970s to the present reveals that men place marriage and family and a warm loving relationship at the top of their list of needs, whereas money and sex rank at the bottom! That's not different from women's responses. What is clear, however, is that men and women don't really understand their own and each other's makeup, so that misinterpretations, mind reading, and hurt feelings abound between them. When they begin to understand each other's views, positive things can happen. Here are some of the major ways the miscommunication gap between the sexes can be bridged by men:

1. When a man comes home from a bad day at work, nerves jangled, his wife can usually sense something is wrong. So she will ask him, "Anything wrong, honey?" And when he says (as he usually does), "Everything's fine," his wife knows he's not telling the truth. So she mind reads and blows it up into a catastrophe, thinking, "He's not telling the truth; he's hiding

something from me. It must be another woman, because otherwise he would tell me the truth." She has added another page to her resentment-collecting file.

These two misunderstand each other. The husband, because of his male programming, feels he always has to appear to be strong and in charge (even when he isn't), thereby giving his wife the wrong impression. His wife, feeling that his lack of honesty is due to something she must have done, convinces herself that he has become involved with another woman. Like grains of sand these misinterpretations, if allowed to mount, can bury a marriage.

I am acutely aware of this fact—so much so that in the early days of my marriage to Pat, when I was working for a firm and would at times come home in disarray, disturbed about office problems, I would make an extra effort to tell her that if I seemed distracted, it had nothing to do with her or our relationship but everything to do with things at the office. This diffused any anxiety and tension that otherwise could have developed between us.

2. Acknowledge your vulnerability. If you have demonstrated your abilities and competence at home and in the business world, acknowledging that you are not always in charge will bring your wife closer to you rather than cause her to think less of you.

I know of many men who have been laid off from their jobs, through no fault of their own, who refrain from telling their wives about the date of their layoff until it happens, because they don't want to worry them. They also fear that their wives will no longer love them, will think their husbands are personal failures because they can't bring home a paycheck. One of our clients so feared that his wife would think him worthless because he no longer had a job that he pretended to go to work every morning for two months after his layoff, until he was found out. His wife was appalled: "Don't you know I love you, not your paycheck? We're in this together, and we'll come out of this rough spot together." And they did.

Expressing your vulnerability in a crisis time will bring your spouse closer to you rather than drive her away. Women want to know how men are feeling as well as how they are behaving.

3. Make certain you and your spouse are speaking the same language. For example, "power" is regarded by men as signifying independence and competitive success. Women, on the other hand, view giving, nurturing, interdependence, and relatedness as signs of strength and achievement, as affirmations of their power.

Both of you can use an agreed-upon definition of power as the expression of one's internal feeling of self-competency. This means that you see yourselves and each other as persons of value and worth in your own right, so that you won't need to play the one-upmanship game in which power is exhibited by exploiting other people, including your spouse. Power then resides in treating each other as interdependent equals who delight in experiencing their relationship as teamwork rather than cut-throat competition.

4. Celebrate and develop the qualities that make men and women fully human to themselves and each other, because these are the qualities needed to create lifelong marital happiness.

For women, this means becoming nurturers who also nurture themselves, who value their intellectual strengths as well as their emotional sensitivity, who take pride in their achievements in the business world and in making the world a better place in which to live, who know the difference between aggressiveness, passivity, and assertiveness and choose to practice assertiveness in their everyday lives, who are comfortable with being women, not clones of men, when they assert their just demand for gender equality.

In turn, men can begin to value themselves for being vulnerable as well as strong, emotional as well as intellectual, companions and colleagues to their wives as well as husbands, friends as well as lovers. In the process, men become whole persons instead of half persons forever searching for their other half.

5. We men and women have much to teach each other. But we cannot do so if we treat each other as enemies. The real enemy here is the cultural conditioning we have received since birth, which steers us on a collision course, one sex against the other. Eliminate that cultural conditioning and substitute gender equality for the inequalities that still inhere in our political system, and many of the issues dividing the sexes will be eliminated.

It is important to remember the achievements of the women's revolution in the short period of its existence. The National Organization for Women was organized in 1966 by thirty women and two men and has had an impact on millions since that time. From its very inception, then, the women's movement included men. And now in the 1990s, with men forming men's groups to help redefine themselves, the future augers well for the ending of the wars, cold and hot, between the sexes.

### Pat's Story

Our work, as Mel has stated, is based on our profound belief that, in order to be successful, any long-term marriage, or any other type of committed relationship, must be lived in practice on the basis of gender equality.

In order to help those couples who come to our center for insights on how to solve their relationship problems, I first had to learn how to help myself gain the knowledge that I would then present to others.

When I was a young woman growing up in the fifties, I certainly was unaware that a feminist revolution would begin a decade later, generating such a positive future for women. Little did I know then how significantly that revolution would affect my own sense of self and personal growth. You see, the cultural climate I grew up in was one of societal conformity; women stayed home and men were the breadwinners. My father was a painter and supervisor on the Golden Gate Bridge in San Francisco. My mother was an accountant who gave up her career when my sister and I were born because society had told her that it was really a "bad thing" for married women to work. I remember that my mother had to struggle with that fact when we were little. She did return to work when we were young but only when my father was in financial straits. She was employed only for very brief periods, because Mom felt she should be at home taking care of her children, as that was her job. But, looking back, I think she was ambivalent.

My mom was a very intelligent person and had a lot to contribute to the world. I feel she would have been happier using her business skills. She was brilliant in mathematics. Before my sister and I were born, she had traveled throughout California, helping various companies with their financial difficulties: she was a troubleshooter. When I was growing up it was very unusual for a mother to work in the business world.

When I was a teenager I remember coming home from school and seeing my mother crying. And I also remember a few times when I awoke suddenly at night: I got up, and my mother was in the kitchen having a cup of tea, and she was crying. I said, "Mother, what's the matter?" Still crying, she said,

"I don't think you kids need me anymore . . . I feel so useless."
And she was sobbing that phrase, "I feel so useless." She continued, "Dad's away at work all the time, and you children are
at high school all day long, so there's nothing for me to do. I'm
in this big house alone, and I just seem to waddle around in it,
and I feel so unhappy—like my role has been taken from me." I
would put my arms around her and say, "Oh, Mother, we'll
always need you. I think you have too much idle time on your
hands, and what you should do is go back to the work that you
did once and were happy doing." She said to me, "Oh, no! I
can't work. That wouldn't make me a good mother and wife."
And so she was between a rock and a hard place. I felt absolutely guilty that I was growing up and away. I felt guilty that I
no longer really did need my mother in the way I needed her
before I went to high school. I tried to give her more of my time,
but my life in high school was bursting with excitement. I was
Girls' President at that time, and I had a lot of committee meet-
ings. I was also very active in the GAA (Girls' Athletic Association), and I sang in the school dance band.

As I recall, my parents expected me to go to a junior college
for two years to take business courses so that if anything happened to the husband I would inevitably marry, I would be able
to go back to work to earn a living. There was never any mention of a four-year college or career for me; I knew from the
time I was very little that I was supposed to get married and
have children and was to expect nothing else from life.

I did go to junior college for one year. I can remember a
male teacher in my advertising class saying, "I know you girls
are just here to find a husband. I hope you do it soon so that I
can get to the serious business at hand, which is teaching the
male students who are preparing themselves for a state college
and careers in business."

As I look back on it now, I get angry. But at the time (you see how brainwashed I was!) his statement did not bother me. I did what was expected of me: I "found" my first husband, married at twenty-one, and had two children by the time I was twenty-three.

I did, however, work for one year as a typist in San Francisco before I married. I loved working. My husband-to-be was in the navy back east at the time, so we had to delay our marriage until his duty was up, which was about one year. But that year was a wonderful one for me. I was so happy to be working and making my own money! I could buy the clothes I wanted for the first time. I felt independent and extremely happy. But he came home, and I got married. He was a Catholic, and his mother insisted that I go through lessons at the Catholic church and convert to Catholicism. (My own mom would encourage me to go to "any" church each Sunday. My mom would call these "many houses under one God." So every Sunday we got to go to a new church—Presbyterian, Methodist, Catholic—a little house of our choosing. We felt a joyous freedom each Sunday.)

When my husband's mother insisted I convert, I did, but I always thought in my mind that "there is one God and many houses." I had a little trouble with the rhythm method (Catholic birth control). I had two babies on that method right in a row, sixteen months apart. I called my children Rhythm 1 and Rhythm 2!

Staying home with my children and playing house full time at age twenty-three was difficult. I loved my children, but I was so young. I laugh today and tell them, "You know, you two really reared me." I was so serious, so dedicated, so untrained; I was so scared I would do something wrong as a mother.

My husband, when he was in the navy, was transferred to Virginia. So there I was alone in Virginia raising my two girls;

my husband was out to sea aboard an aircraft carrier for six weeks at a time. I craved adult companionship. I didn't realize how much work there was to do for two children—I was always folding diapers, washing diapers, diapers stacked up to the ceiling—as I look back, I don't know how I did it. I would play a guessing game trying to figure out the meaning of their discomforts until the children learned to talk. I would accuse myself of having something wrong with me—I should be happier. Oh, how I craved adult companionship! That made me feel doubly guilty, because I just felt it was all work and no play. In fact, after four years in Virginia, we finally came home to California. I had a talk with my sister, and I said to her, "I'm not happy." And she said, "You're not happy doing what?" And I replied, "Not happy just taking care of the children and staying home. I wish I could work too." And she looked at me as if I had slapped her in the face. She said, "My God, you wouldn't want to work." And I said, "Yes, I really feel I'd like to get back to what I was doing before." But she just thought that would be a disgrace; even my friends felt the way my sister did.

When my children were about four and five, I used to read advertisements in our hometown paper and knew I was qualified for some of the jobs listed. I would take the children in the backseat of my car, and I would buy them some goodies and say, "Now, you have to stay in the car while Mommy goes to this interview. Mommy can see your heads, so don't get out of the car, and I will be no more than twenty minutes." Then I would go to the interview, and, sure enough, I would get the job. I would lie and say, "No I don't have any children," because companies in the fifties would not hire a woman with young children. I would get hired and work for a week; then one of the children would get sick, and I would have to call and quit. Then I would do the whole thing again in six months. I'd last about a week in a job, and then the same thing would happen.

When the couples I knew in high school and college, who now were married to each other, got together, the women would talk to one another, and the men would congregate separately. The conversation for women would be about children, their husbands, their household duties, and so on. The men, on the other hand, would talk about politics, golf, their jobs. I found the politics the men talked about more interesting than women's household woes. I would move to the men's group and assert myself and my beliefs. Some of the men were quite conservative, and so we would have some heated discussions.

My mom and dad and his brothers and sisters would visit us every weekend in Mill Valley. They loved to talk politics. My father was a strong labor union member. He and Mom both went through the depression of 1929, and they remembered lean days when an employer had the power to hire workers for a pittance. My father always worked for fair employment practices. He'd had to quit school in the seventh grade at the age of twelve when his father died and as the oldest (he had three sisters and a brother) he had to go to work to support the family. It was always his passion to fight hard for the laboring force.

My mom was educated and taught my dad to read. She was his teacher all his life. My mom would study with my dad, and if they didn't know something, they would look it up in the Lincoln Library. It was truly a course in political science each and every night. My sister and I would participate. My father would not only discuss with us and read to us about politics, he would expose the bias in magazines and newspaper articles.

I can remember that when I was fourteen I used to ride my bicycle toward the one large private college in town. And as I was bicycling around the college, I would say to myself, "This is a gorgeous place. This is so neat! I feel such a desire to go to college here." But then I would think, "Yes, but you have to have a lot of money to attend this college, and you have to be highly intelligent. They would find out that I'm not." (I got Bs and Cs in high school—I had too good a time to really sit down and study.) So I would say to myself, "You know, this is an impossible dream. Yes, I can enjoy riding around the campus like this, but a poor kid like me will never get a chance to go here. Never in a million years." But I would crane my neck to see the students, to see if they really were so different from me. And when I did see a student coming out of the library or class, I would stare and follow her. In her uniform, she looked almost holy. I had such a desire to go to that college that when I discussed the idea with my second husband, Mel, and he said of course it would be possible for me to begin in this college, I was just delighted. In my freshman year, I felt as though I were walking on water. It seemed like the best thing that had ever happened to me.

The women's movement in the late sixties freed me of my belief that I was a bad wife and mother who was guilty for wanting more out of life. I started to question the fairness of the men, like my husband, making all the major decisions in women's lives. I was very unhappy in my marriage, and divorce was now something that society sanctioned. My first husband would not communicate with me, and he would always use the excuse that he had to work extra hours to be alone on the weekends, away from home. In 1969 I told him I wanted a divorce.

My children went through the sixties in San Francisco—in fact, Janis Joplin was my eldest daughter's heroine! I can remember her telling me that the life I was living with my first husband was so materialistic and phony and had to be changed, that the whole society stinks, and that her generation was going to make a better world. There was, along with the naïveté, more than a grain of truth in what she said!

Looking back on my own personal development, I feel as if I am every woman who comes to see me at our center:

1. There's the divorced woman that I once was, thirty-six years old, wanting to get the college degree she never had but afraid she's not intelligent enough to do so. I can tell her that's exactly how I felt when I returned to college at the age of thirty-seven and that we older women were very highly regarded by the teachers. In fact, we were called DARs, shorthand for "damn average raisers," because we were so smart. We had the advantage over the younger students because we approached school more seriously—working on our reports intensively, diligently absorbing our class work, and never cutting classes. We were not there to party and date, which deflects so many younger students from their courses.

2. There are the nonassertive women who find it difficult to nurture themselves (there are so many of them even today!). I can remember how unassertive I was for so many years of my life before I learned the exciting fact that any woman who wishes to change her behavior can become assertive. It seemed as though from the time I was old enough to walk I could never say no to any request made of me. If a friend called me and said, "Would you mind watching my children on Saturday, because I have this engagement I forgot all about and I can't get a babysitter?" I would always say yes even though I had more important things to do. I would do things I really didn't want to do but would take them on because I didn't want to be unhelpful. I would always put what I wanted to do second and help others first.

When I was a homemaker on a very limited budget, I would get into trouble when salesmen came to the door selling magazines or books. I would stand outside the door and listen to their spiels and think, "Golly, they're trying to get through college, and they need this subscription. And the booklet is so interesting. And the magazine is so great." So I'd sign up for whatever it was, and when my husband got home, he was furious with me for buying something we didn't need. But I just couldn't say no, whether it was traveling salesmen or phone solicitors. I just couldn't hang up on anyone, so I would listen for hours on end to someone's hard-luck story. I continue to believe it's important to help other people, but sometimes helping others is not helpful to oneself.

I remember a turning point when I became assertive. It sounds like a very small step, but it was a giant one at the time. I was in a long line at a bank and was pressed for time. When I finally got right up to the bank teller, a woman came in on my right and said, "I'm in such a hurry. I know you don't mind if I go first." I looked at her and said, "I beg your pardon. I've been here in this line for over an hour. And I feel that it is my turn to be waited on by the teller. I'm sorry, I cannot help you." I felt my knees start to buckle, because this was the first time I had ever said no to someone's unreasonable request of me.

Ordinarily, my tendency would have been to say, "Of course, go ahead." But then I would have gotten angry, too. I would have taken the car out of the bank lot and gone a mile a minute because I was so angry over what had happened. This time, however, my stopping her freed me from letting that small injustice darken my entire day. It was as though a black cloud disappeared, and the day became sunny for me.

It's still typical for many women today not to understand that when something happens that hurts them, makes them feel bad, or greatly inconveniences them, it's their perfect right to state outright, "I feel uncomfortable with your action or last statement." I mean, just saying that simple phrase, "I feel uncomfortable" can open up a dialogue in which a woman can be heard and get her needs met. Working with women, I attempt to help empower them to the point where they indeed feel they have the right to assert themselves in this manner.

3. There are the women who have no understanding of how powerful women are and therefore have little self-esteem.

Until the advent of the women's movement I felt the same way. But when I saw women like Gloria Steinem and Betty Friedan taking leadership roles in society, when I saw women in the media (like Oprah Winfrey and Jane Pauley) outperforming men, I started to question the myth that women were the second sex. I began reading books such as Betty Friedan's *The Feminine Mystique* and Simone de Beauvoir's *The Second Sex*. And the book that was my greatest eye-opener—a book I recommend to every woman I work with—was *For Her Own Good,* by Barbara Ehrenreich and Deirdre English (New York: Doubleday Anchor, 1979). In that book, I learned the following history of my sex:

In Europe in the sixteenth and seventeenth centuries, before many of our ancestors migrated to America, thousands of women were executed or burned at the stake because they were considered too powerful in the communities in which they lived. This infamous practice continued in the Salem witchcraft trials here in the United States. These powerful women were healers and midwives and also performed abortions. They knew the healing properties of plants and trees, the value of anti-inflammatory herbal medicine. They used painkillers and digestive remedies that men knew little or nothing about. This frightened the monks and priests of the time, who thought that women were trying to be "more Godly than God" by using their "mystical powers," so they were condemned to death as "witches."

In colonial times, women's work was essential for family survival. As *For Her Own Good* points out:

It was the wife's duty, with the assistance of daughters and women servants, to plant the vegetable garden, breed the poultry, and care for the dairy cattle. She transformed milk into cream, butter and cheese, and butchered live-stock as well as cooked the meals. Along with her daily chores the husbandwoman slated, pickled, preserved, and manufactured enough beer and cider to see the family through the winter. . . .

To clothe the colonial population, women not only plied the needle, but operated wool carders and spinning wheels—participated in the manufacture of thread, yarn and cloth as well as apparel. Her handwrought candles lit the house; medicines of her manufacture restored the family to health; her home-made soap cleansed her home and family.

In the nineteenth century the power of women was severely diminished by the formation of the American Medical Association in 1847. The male doctors who formed the association had felt threatened by the activities of women healers and decided to make medicine an exclusive male prerogative. The AMA was the perfect instrument by which to attain that end.

Despite such setbacks, women's power continued to assert itself in every branch of society. In the nineteenth century women like Elizabeth Cady Stanton and Harriet Beecher Stowe fought for women's suffrage and an end to slavery. In the twentieth century, heroines like Nobel scientist Marie Curie demonstrated women's intellectual powers. There was Helen Keller, deaf and blind since birth, who became an outstanding fighter for the disabled and the poor. The world of philosophy was enriched by the work of Simone de Beauvoir, while painters like Georgia O'Keeffe and Frida Kahlo graced twentieth-century art with their genius. The American theater would be much diminished had Lillian Hellman not written her plays. And let's not forget the internationally famous writer and pre–World War I political activist Rebecca West. It was she who wrote sardonically in 1913, "I myself have never been able to find out precisely what feminism is. I only know that people call me a feminist whenever I express sentiments that differentiate me from a doormat." I don't think that most women know what feminism is. To me, a feminist is a person who gives herself the ability to grow, to stretch herself, to follow her dreams, and to reach her goals.

In my practice, I try to help women get in touch with the very real personal power they have to influence their relationships positively. And, given that women are 51 percent of the population, we can be an effective force for remedying society's injustices against us. There are so many injustices: for instance, women have no guarantee of maternity leave, paid or otherwise. It's ironic that the only other industrialized country in the world that doesn't guarantee maternity leave is the nation of South Africa. Women still make only seventy cents for every dollar men earn. Why, the average female high school graduate earns less than the average male elementary school graduate! And sexual harassment on the job has always been an occupational hazard for females.

Mary Catherine Farley, a family relations lawyer who practices in Sausalito, California, has had extensive experience with the issue of sexual harassment and how it infects and undermines male-female relationships. Here are her comments:

> What we see in the issue of sexual harassment is that it cuts through to all of the other human relationships men have with the other half of the human race. It is one way of expressing the basic disparity of understanding between the sexes.
>
> Sexual harassment has a tie-in with a man's relationship with women outside of the workplace. It seems an intellectual and emotional possibility that a man who

would harass a woman in the workplace would also act
hostilely toward the women in his personal life: he would
also see his elderly mother as disposable, his wife as
divorceable, his sisters as second-class in the family,
and his female children as less valuable than his male
children.

Sexual activity does not belong in the workplace: we're
there, men and women both, to do a job, get paid, and
go home. It's the abuse of power, exercised to protect
male territory in the workplace. The minute you see a
woman climbing telephone poles, being hired by a gas
and electric company as a troubleshooter, being admitted
to the carpenters' or plumbers' unions, she becomes a
threat to what was previously male territory. And if she is
as good or better than a man in those jobs, she may dis-
place him or his brother or his buddy.

Men in the workplace try to keep their power by
patronizing women, by stereotyping and demeaning them
as nothing more than sex objects, by making them feel
like helpless victims without recourse. That intimidation
can take subtle as well as grossly obvious forms. For
example, I was in court with a very competent woman
attorney who wore very attractive feminine clothes that
were appropriate for work. In the courtroom the male
judge referred to this woman not by her name, but by the
term "lace curtains." He said, "Where's 'lace curtains'?"
when he was looking for her. By that characterization he
had squashed her mentality into a symbol that was a putdown of Irish women, since the term "lace curtains"
implies a person is pretentious and self-centered. He char-
acterized her by her dress rather than her abilities. This
extraordinarily capable female lawyer, who persuasively

argued her case, would never be able to penetrate his stereotype of her.

You know, there really is not that much difference between sexual harassment and rape. Both involve an abuse of power: it's only a matter of gradation.

If you ask why a woman will stay in an abusive relationship, such as in a job or marriage, it's because she doesn't have the power or knowledge of how to extricate herself from it. Such women are dependent for their economic survival in both the workplace and marriage, particularly if they have children. I don't think women are born victims. It's true that there are women who will trade their sexual favors to get ahead, or just to survive. They are victimized. For they are using the only tool of power they have at their disposal—their ability to grant or deny sexual favors—to attain economic survival. There are a lot of women in their marriages who prostitute themselves to get their daily bread and sustenance for their children—and they get nothing more out of their marriages. Is legalized prostitution any different? Both involve abuse of power, where the men grant economic survival to the women in exchange for sexual favors. Once they begin to know about their rights, that they have more personal power than they ever suspected they had to lead happier lives, remarkable things happen. Never underestimate the ability of women to make positive changes in their lives once they understand that they have been unwilling victims and no longer need to play that role.

I don't want to leave you with the impression that men and women are natural enemies. That's not true at all. In fact, I am very optimistic about the future of the relationships between the sexes. For more and more men and women are beginning to ask the question that really counts, and that is, "Am I first a human being and then male or female?" Both men and women are now engaged in the process of becoming more fully human, more rounded human beings. And to that end the positive stake for men in supporting women's struggle for gender equality is enormous.

The joy of women experiencing real equality in the workplace and at home and the joy of men nurturing the tender, empathic, cooperative side of their nature—this is what I see as the wave of the future. It's a future men and women should both fight for!

Since our objective in writing this book is to help improve marital relationships, the spotlight must focus not only on each individual's responsibility to improve a marriage, it must also focus on society and the way in which it undermines rather than reinforces that possibility. Mary Catherine Farley has eloquently outlined how sexual harassment intensifies male-female relationship difficulties. Unfortunately, there are many other societal problems that escalate marital distress:

1. Without a decent, stable income, marriages are more likely to fall apart than to become more loving. We are experiencing the worst depression since the 1930s, with more than 10 million men and women unemployed. In the words of district executive director of the Catholic Family Services of New Haven, Connecticut (reported in the *New York Times,* 13 April 1992), chronic unemployment among the middle class is contributing to family breakdowns, vanishing spouses, substance abuse "and a horrible increase in domestic violence."

2. The Children's Defense Fund revealed in the *New York Times,* 15 April 1992, that young families today (with a family head younger than age thirty) have incomes 32 percent lower than their counterparts seventeen years ago—and 40 percent of them and their children now live in poverty. Marian Wright Edelman, president of the fund, stated that this appalling situation results in "more substance abuse, more crime, more violence, more teen pregnancy, more racial tension, more envy, more despair, and more cynicism—a long-term economic and social disaster."

3. Our society's priorities demonstrate that the leaders of our country only give cynical lip service to nurturing family and marital life. How else can one explain the fact that we are still spending almost 300 billion dollars a year on military equipment in the face of a nonexistent cold war, and can readily vote appropriations of 100 billion dollars and more for helping savings and loan operators who have advantaged only their own greed? On the other hand, our politicians complain that the more modest amounts needed to shore up out schools, libraries, child and health care, and housing needs are impossible to supply.

In the face of this outrageous state of affairs, it is a testament to the commitment to love, marriage, and the family that so many couples remain together in these times. Given society's seemingly determined attempt to destroy family life by distorting the priorities of our country, every couple that validates marriage rather than divorce deserves a salute of honor!

## Chapter Five

# The Good-Enough-Parent Marriage

The third marriage of your marriage deals with parenthood. It is the third because couples today usually focus on stabilizing their careers or jobs before having children. Conceiving a first child in one's late twenties or thirties has become the norm rather than the exception.

In the 1950s and 1960s, if a woman didn't have a child by the age of thirty, the chances were she never would. Climbing the career ladder by men was combined with having an almost instant family after marriage; usually three or four children by the time a couple reached thirty.

By contrast, most women today will have their first child after thirty, and the average family consists of two children instead of four. In the 1950s and 1960s, the husband was usually the sole wage earner, while today the two-paycheck family is the norm.

Childless couples in our society are still the exception rather than the rule, but it is a more acceptable choice than ever. People today have many options other than parenthood. Fulfilling marriages can and do exist in which both partners feel that they neither desire children nor possess the capacity to contend with the demands and discomforts that parenthood inevitably entails. However, couples who feel this way should consider the possibility that their decision may be right for them now, but wrong later. Circumstances do change; they themselves may one day develop the very desire for children that they don't feel today. This is confirmed by the thousands of men who have undergone vasectomy reversals now that microsurgery techniques are available for that purpose. Couples who choose not to have children might well keep all their options open, including the right to change their minds.

Many infertile couples who want children can now realize their dreams by means of in vitro fertilization or through contracting with surrogate birth mothers. And single parents and nonmarried domestic partners can now adopt with less hassle.

Most married couples dream of having a nice cozy family of four—two lovely children and two proud parents. This dream arises out of the best of impulses, and it can work if its implications are freely discussed and the decision to begin a family is unconditionally agreed to by both husband and wife. They are about to experience one of life's profoundest adventures. This kind of mutual decision arises out of all that is best in each of them: the desire for a purpose in life beyond themselves; the desire to create; the desire to leave a legacy of significant consequence on this earth, which they must later leave; and the desire to expand the love they have for each other in the love they will give their child.

The good-enough-parent marriage begins at the point when a couple decides to have a child, not when the child is born. How you view the idea of parenthood will shape your attitudes and actions toward your baby once he or she arrives. Is the motivator "Let's have a baby because all of our friends are doing it?" A desire for a symbol authenticating your adulthood? The need for someone to provide you with the round-the-clock love you never had? A validation of your personal worth from someone other than yourself? Is it to satisfy your spouse, who really wants a child, while you have grave reservations about it? Is it to save your troubled marriage, because you think a child will bring you and your spouse closer together?

A decision based on unconditional love for the expected baby will provide a perspective for experiencing the child with joy and delight, planting the seeds of a healthy self-image in the child from birth. The inevitable disruptions and frustrations involved in parenting will then be taken in stride. When the decision is based on other reasons or motives, self-created difficulties will arise: your own conflicts will interfere with the child's developing self-image. Very early in life he or she may develop a sense of not belonging, a feeling of not being wanted, not being valued as an individual as well as the flesh and blood of mother and father. Twenty years later that child may say, as so many do, "I never really felt I was loved for who I was; I was only loved because of what I could do for Mom and Dad."

All prospective parents, no matter how well prepared for parenthood, will experience a tempest of shocks and surprises once the infant arrives. In fact, shocks and surprises can begin during pregnancy. A husband, while happily anticipating the blessed event, may experience occasional fear and depression as he sees his wife becoming more internally centered: the love and excitement she once felt for him may seem to him to shift to the fetus growing inside her. When asked to feel the baby kicking inside the womb, a husband may feel pride and love but also a fear that he may no longer be number one in his marriage. He may see confirmation of this in the decline in their sexual relationship over the nine months of pregnancy. His wife may reinforce his feeling of being second-best if she views her changed figure during pregnancy as a sign of her own unattractiveness, rather than as the normal shape of a mother-to-be.

A husband may have pseudopregnancy feelings—a nausea similar to morning sickness or stomach pains, or even put on excess weight around his middle. These surprising things may be positive signs of empathy with the woman he loves or negative signs indicating that the child will be an unwelcome intruder into his marriage. It all depends on the extent to which the decision to have a child arises from a mature need to participate in one of life's greatest experiences or from a misguided attempt to obtain instant happiness or solve a marital problem.

If there is one guarantee the birth of a child can provide, it is that his or her presence will not solve a marital problem or provide instant happiness. To the contrary, couples who see a child as a solution to problems are most likely to break up. The child becomes the scissors that sever the marital bond rather than its cement. Infants initially intensify old problems and create new ones. At birth they are a mountain of demands, uproars, frustrations, disruptions, responsibilities, and obligations.

Even those couples who have made all the "right" moves in anticipation of their infant's birth are liable to be surprised and rather shaken by the unexpected disarray in their daily lives and emotions that the "little stranger" in their house gives rise to. And a little stranger he or she is, regardless of all the child-care books the parents might have read or all the preparation in a Lamaze class they may have undergone. Such a husband and wife might have had a "peak experience" through the awareness and the creative power of their child's actual birth. The new mother may feel the greatest surge of warmth and tenderness spreading within her when she cuddles and nurses the baby. And the new father may experience a similar delight in holding the infant and observing him or her in voraciously contented suckling or sleeping. All these experiences might have been anticipated and realized—but not the onslaught of the unexpected.

For during the first months, an infant is a bottomless pit of needs. Who would have thought that being a mother would mean all work and no play? Twenty-four hours of each day. Why does the child have to have a bowel movement a half hour after you've bathed, powdered, and bedded him or her—and just when you're ready to relax for a few minutes in front of the TV? Why does the doorbell or telephone always have to ring as soon as the baby is ready to fall asleep, so that the crying begins again? Is the baby trying to capture first place in the *Guinness Book of Records* for the number of bowel movements or the number of soggy diapers each day? And is that another rash you see on the baby's bottom?

Then there is the concern over proper room temperature and drafts that may result in a cold or fever. There are the bottles and nipples that need sterilizing and the formulas that have to be made. The bottle may be too hot or too cold, and while you correct it, the baby is crying from hunger. Danger is always lurking around the house. You may feel guilty to discover strands of hair from your head entangled around the neck or fingers or toes of your child, for those seemingly harmless strands could stop the infant's circulation. The stories you hear about crib deaths escalate your fears. Your child may be allergic to the formula you were giving him or her. Watch out for baby's toenails and fingernails, which must be cut lest the baby bruises itself! Be sure to take care that those tiny, fragile fingers and toes are not hurt when you do the cutting. And just when things seem to settle down, there are the unexpected colds, high fevers, and colic that may keep you up all night and make you believe that for the rest of your life you will never again be permitted a good night's sleep.

Perhaps the biggest initial shock is the realization that there is a gigantic communication gap between you and your newborn that you will have to bridge. Your infant speaks to you in the language of crying and other sounds and facial and body gestures. Initially, it's a foreign language. There are cries, and there are cries: "I've just soiled my diapers, clean me!" "I have an air bubble, burp me!" or "I have a rash, powder me!" "Don't leave me; if I'm left alone I'll die." Sometimes it's a cry that asserts an infant's personality or a coo or gurgle of contentment. The grimace on his or her face may mean a passing of gas or a response to the environment; body squirms and kicks may mean discomfort or high spirits. In any case, a trial-and-error deciphering of this language takes time, and feelings of confusion, incompetency, or ignorance may occasionally overwhelm you. And just when you become accustomed to your child's schedule of demands and have accommodated yourself to your child's routine and rhythm, teething begins—and with it a new cycle of crying, discomfort, and disruption.

The degree to which new parents understand that the unexpected is to be expected during the first months after the baby's birth, the degree to which they realize that no one can ever be a "perfect" parent, but that they have the capacity to cope with the unexpected, will determine the kind of basis they establish for a subsequent loving enjoyment of their child and other children to come. Freud himself said parenting is a most imperfect profession. Being a "good enough" parent is good enough.

Moving from being a couple to becoming parents will dramatically change your relationship to each other. In the past, you have been lovers and career persons and defined your relationship in terms of being husband and wife. Now your sense of self expands to include becoming mother and father. Perhaps in no other of the seven marriages of your marriage will you and your spouse find as much potential for the development of difficult triangles and mutual development challenges. Becoming "mother" and "father" requires viewing yourselves in a whole new light. Marriages are at great risk of foundering on the rocks of divorce if the new triangles and challenges are not skillfully resolved.

## *The Typical Marriage Triangles in the Good-Enough-Parent Marriage*

### *The Infertility Triangle*

Couples who desire a natural birth may be profoundly disappointed to find out they are infertile. They may feel depressed after spending thousands of dollars in fertility treatments that yielded no positive result. This is a perfect ground for nourishing resentments and blame-making. A husband may blame his wife for being incapable of conceiving. A wife may blame her husband for causing her to have an abortion earlier in her life when it was possible for her to conceive, or she may accuse him of having an excessively low sperm count. (Statistically, 50 percent of infertility cases originate in the wife and the other 50 percent in the husband.) If these accusations and resentments remain unresolved and continue to fester, they can become an infertility triangle of estrangement and alienation, often leading to divorce.

### *The Betrayal Triangle*

Couples can trap themselves into an "I would rather be right than happy" mode of behavior by agreeing early in their marriage (usually when they are still in their twenties) "never" to have any children. Then five or ten years later, the wife may turn around and say she wants a child before her biological clock stops ticking. The husband may protest, saying she has "betrayed" their agreement, because his desire not to have children hasn't changed. She says she has a right to change her mind; he says she is "wrong" to violate their early agreement. Sometimes it is the husband who has changed his mind, while the wife is still adamant about not having children. In either case, the result is the same: if they become locked into a rigid belief in their own "rightness," a betrayal triangle will result, with each spouse considering the other untrustworthy. More and more of their time will be spent collecting injustices instead of concentrating on the kind things they could do for each other. The acid of feeling betrayed will corrode the marriage if the couple persists in this behavior.

### The My-Infant-My-Enemy Triangle

Young people who were fed a steady diet of TV-family stories, old films, and sentimental novels may carry into their lives the dream that having children soon after marriage will supply them with all the happiness they will ever need. Very many couples who marry in their teens or early twenties are gripped by the fantasy that they will create the ideal family. A teenage wife, in particular, may urgently desire a child to fulfill her vision that a happy, carefree, tractable infant will cater to her needs the instant he or she emerges from her womb. Her child, she thinks, will be her plaything, will be her validation that she is now a valuable and important person, will give her all the love and affection she never had.

The child will eat and sleep on schedule and while awake will devote all his or her time to giving mother pleasure. But when reel life turns into real life, she may feel betrayed. How unfair it is! She was the one who needed the nurturing, but her infant has turned the tables and become a bottomless pit of demands on her instead. As a result of this turnabout, she is liable to transform her child into her enemy. She has created a triangle in which the third side of the triangle is her own baby; all her energies are focused on the child, and her husband is no longer number one in her eyes.

Gored by her frustrations, her lack of patience, her inability to foresee a time when the incessant demands of early infanthood will end, she may begin to view her totally vulnerable infant as a greedy monster who is devouring the very substance of her life. In fact, murderous thoughts about how nice it would be to dispatch the infant back to the nothingness from which it came may flit through her mind. And when she thinks these unthinkable thoughts, she may feel guilty and fearful and lash out at her husband in an attempt to rid herself of her guilt for having these feelings. Both may see each other as the ultimate cause of their discontent, exchanging charges of "if it weren't for you, I'd never be in this mess." If the husband was a victim of the same dream his wife had, and is equally incapable of becoming a responsible parent, a breakup is in sight. Couples who marry in their late teens or early twenties and have a child shortly thereafter stand a more than 50 percent chance of divorcing in the first five years of their marriage.

This tendency to create an enemy out of a helpless infant is not limited to couples who marry early, although it happens most frequently with them. More mature couples, aware of child-care literature and feeling rather sophisticated and intelligent, will on occasion fall prey to the same kind of attitude. Unless you are a saint, how could it be otherwise? A wife who had been a career person may feel trapped and isolated and demeaned in her role as a permanent baby-tender. A husband who happily attended a Lamaze course may later feel comparably trapped by the escalating economic obligations that an addition to the family causes. He may feel deprived of the freedom to socialize, to take weekend trips, to make love with his wife spontaneously. However, knowing that children go through phases of development, that the round-the-clock demands of an infant will pass, prevents the my-infant-my-enemy triangle from congealing. Love triumphs over anger and frustration as the child grows older.

## The My-Infant-My-Lover Triangle

A reverse image of the my-infant-my-enemy triangle is the my-infant-my-lover triangle. Many parents fall in love with their infants at first sight. From the moment of birth, they see the infant as beautiful and perfect. The child's cries are like the sound of music. No demand of the infant is excessive; it's a privilege to be able to attend to every single one of them. Talking to the infant, singing, cooing, holding, cuddling, watching, and kissing is an endless source of satisfaction.

It sounds fine, but something may be wrong with all this bliss. For usually it is only one of the parents who feels so totally involved and committed. The other may have more ambivalent feelings. Most often the totally involved parent is the mother, but it can be the father. In this triangle, the infant becomes the number one love, and the spouse is demoted to number two.

This triangle can develop even in a fundamentally sound marriage. A wife may be so delighted with her new role as mother that she unintentionally overlooks the needs of her husband. The husband, loving his child, may be uncertain of his role as a parent and need direction about how he can share in the responsibilities and joys of parenthood. In this scenario, his feelings that he is the left-out member of the family need not create a permanent triangle. Open discussion and sharing of information can solve the problem.

In other cases, the solution is not so simple. A triangle of this type can last a lifetime if it arises from a troubled marriage. A wife will try to satisfy her own needs, which she feels her husband is not filling, by switching her primary attention to her child. Her child, at least, responds positively to her, even if her husband doesn't. Besides, it is an indirect way of punishing her husband: if he feels neglected, it serves him right! The husband, in turn, may feel envious of the affection and attention his child is receiving and transform the vulnerable infant into a love rival. Why should the child receive all the love and affection, the warmth, tenderness, and attention he, as a husband, feels he is entitled to? He may see his wife breast-feeding and envy the intense close relationship and gratification his wife and child derive from each other. He may find himself thinking, "Her breast is for lovemaking, yet here she is giving it to the child instead of me. How dare she!" He may develop an antipathy for his own child that may permanently damage his subsequent relationship with him or her. And he may look elsewhere for the love he lacks.

Role-reversal versions of this triangle are not uncommon. In recent years we have come to recognize that the nurturing instinct is not reserved for women only. In a troubled marriage, a husband with a strong nurturing instinct may become the child's "lover." The wife then becomes second-best in the marriage and may feel the same anger and resentment that a man may feel—and also search for love outside the marriage.

If this triangle is perpetuated and never resolved, the dreadful possibility of incest exists.

## *The Somebody-Else-Will-Love-Me Triangle*

When they harden into permanent attitudes, the my-infant-my-enemy and the my-infant-my-lover triangles can precipitate extramarital affairs. The spouse who feels second-best in the relationship may become self-righteous and operate out of a feeling of "I'll show you that somebody else will love me, because it's clear you no longer do." And a spouse who is determined to find someone else will find that someone else. But an affair triggered by the birth of a child is usually unsatisfying. It is more often than not a cry for help to remedy a situation that is out of control, rather than a genuine desire for divorce or remarriage. Though an affair may be both exciting and sexually gratifying, it is often fraught with guilt and fear (particularly in light of AIDS and other sexually transmitted diseases). And it further erodes whatever trust was left in the marriage.

It is true that for some people an affair can be a catalyst—the excuse needed to get a divorce. These are the people who have come to realize that they are not fit for parenthood, possibly not even for a childless marriage. They often make little attempt to hide their infidelity, and when the spouse discovers the affair, they opt for divorce after a feeble attempt at reconciliation. The "other woman" or "other man" in the affair is often just a passing interest that enables the divorce to happen. (Frequently such an affair ends when the marriage ends.)

# *Your Mutual Development Challenges*

The mutual development challenges faced by you and your spouse in your two previous marriages of your marriage concerned accommodating yourselves to your new marital roles and then to your roles as career persons in ways that moved you closer together rather than farther apart. The challenges in your good-enough-parent marriage are of a different order, because the focus of attention now shifts to your new roles as mother and father. The challenges are these:

1. **The challenge to differentiate your child from your spouse and to see your spouse as a separate individual as well as part of a threesome.**

That helpless, vulnerable infant who is totally dependent on you for survival is neither a sexual rival nor a substitute for your husband or wife. Neither is he or she a cruel, insatiably demanding monster. An infant is just a tiny creature who will grow up to be independent and unique rather than a carbon copy of you or your spouse. An infant is entitled to be loved by you as a child rather than as an adult.

That your spouse's needs may at many times differ and clash with yours owing to the demands of parenting signifies your separateness and uniqueness rather than an attack on your personhood. This challenge requires both of you to expand your capacity to share your feelings honestly, in such ways that the differences and clashes can be understood as separate viewpoints rather than as evil attacks. In so doing, you can find cooperative ways to minimize difficulties.

2. **The challenge to incorporate into your personality a mature image of yourself as a mother or father in addition to your images of yourself in your other roles in life.**

This means accepting your new responsibilities of parenthood as natural and normal consequences of the decision to have a child, rather than as signs that you are a victim of unfair circumstances. If you and your wife, prior to the birth of your child, enjoyed taking trips together every weekend, you may find yourself telling your spouse that having a child will not interfere with that. You might consider yourself to be the same person you were before to the birth of your baby—a married man with no responsibilities or obligations that might interfere with the personal pleasures you had in the past with your wife. After all, you might say to your wife, the baby can stay with the grandparents, who would love to take care of him or her every weekend, or we can always hire a baby-sitter. You might find yourself surprised and resentful when your wife turns down your invitation because she now prefers to remain close to her baby. You will then have failed to take on a mature image of yourself as a father in place of the my-only-responsibility-is-to-my-own-pleasure image that you had prior to the child's birth. You may then misinterpret your wife's refusal to leave the child with others each weekend as a sign that she no longer loves you as much as she once did, and become angry.

You need to revise your image of yourself and your wife. You are still the most important adult in your wife's life, but now that she is a mother, another kind of love has emerged in her: maternal love. This new love demands that old ways of relating, ways that did not include the need to nurture and care for an infant, must now be adapted to parenthood. A new aspect of your wife's potential as a human being has emerged that demands fulfillment: the mothering part. You, in turn, must permit that new part of *your* self—fatherhood—to emerge so that you and your wife can mutually enjoy your child as an integral part of your new family rather than as an interloper.

A mature image of yourselves as a mother and a father requires a greater understanding of the sexual consequences of parenthood. For example, when, as a husband, you see your wife spending so much time loving and caring for the baby in that first year, understand that she is really loving a part of you in that baby, because the baby was made from both of you. In those first months after birth, your wife is physically depleted and needs time for physical self-renewal; her sexual need for you as a husband at that time is more like a banked fire than a roaring flame. If you act like an involved, nurturing, patient father rather than a rejected spouse, the sexual love between the two of you will again flame up once those demanding early months end.

You may experience other sexual surprises with the birth of a baby. Suddenly the two of you become "mother" and "father" as well as "husband" and "wife." At the unconscious level these are two highly charged words filled with sexual connotations.

Dr. Ralph Greenson once described in a lecture how the words *mother* and *father* can affect a couple's behavior toward each other once they have a child:

> Your young lover, it occurs to you, is now a mother, or a father, and how can you get passionate and have sex with somebody's mother or father? That is incestuous and forbidden. You may laugh at this, but think of the marriages you know where, in the early years, pre-maritally and before the baby was born, there was great passion and sex, and suddenly it stops, because the partner is a parent-mother, a father. My God! Sex isn't possible. Imagine what happens later, when the woman you're married to becomes a grandmother, or you become a grandfather! You go to bed and have sex with a grand-mother? Or a grandfather? The answer is yes, if you survive all these things, you will.

### 3. The challenge to create a new balance in your life.

The total neediness of a newborn child does not last for-ever. By the end of the first year, routines and schedules and the rhythm of waking and sleeping are fairly well regularized. The pleasures of seeing your child become increasingly responsive and competent more than make up for your sacrifices. But a child-centered life—to the exclusion of adult pleasures—will make you both cranky and dull, boring to yourselves, boring to each other. Adult-centered pleasures need to be incorporated into your lives: a walk in the park, a candlelight dinner, a film or concert, sports, or a weekend alone together—all demand consideration, because the burdens of child care in the earliest years can dampen your interest in your spouse. Your good-enough-parent marriage requires that you regain your sense of humor; the heavy burdens of the early years of parenting need to be balanced against the perspective that life need not be that serious all the time and that kids are funny people, too.

### 4. The challenge to revise and expand your perspective on life.

Your child is not only the evidence of a new life on earth; he or she is also a shadow of your own mortality. You come to realize that you need to make the most of your limited time on this planet. Because a child moves through stages of development from infancy to adulthood, you need to develop receptive and constructive responses to life's changes. Your realization that you yourself experienced the same developmental changes that your child will experience confirms that nothing lasts forever. In the face of present difficulties, it is important to cultivate the long view that "this too shall pass."

### 5. The challenge to refrain from regarding your newborn child as a carbon copy of one of your own or your spouse's relatives.

Your child may indeed be "the spitting image" of a relative, but such physical resemblance is inconsequential rather than significant. The physical resemblance has nothing whatsoever to do with your child's personality traits, intelligence, interests, or behavior. But you may unconsciously limit your child's personality and abilities if you assume that, because your child resembles that relative in a physical way, he or she must also resemble that relative in every other way. For example, if your child looks like your sister who never went to college because she wasn't interested in intellectual pursuits, you may unconsciously encourage your child's nonintellectual interests and downplay her intellectual capacity, thus inhibiting her growth potential. You may also impose upon yourself a preference or dislike for your child depending upon whether your feelings about the relative your child resembles are positive or negative. Either way, your relationship with your child will suffer, for you will fail to value your child for the unique individual he or she is.

6. **The challenge to overcome constructively your intense ambivalence concerning your need to work and your need to mother if you are a career-oriented wife with children.**

A career, or babies, or both? Nobody would have asked this question a few decades ago. In your mother's generation, the answer was given by society, not by the women themselves: babies first, of course. A career was considered an aberrant indulgence or even an unimaginable option. For better or worse, society provided a clear-cut guideline for "normal" behavior. At that time, if a woman with children worked, she was labeled a "bad mother" not only by her neighbors but by herself. A working mother ordinarily worked out of necessity, but knew she "should" be home with her babies instead. Society told her that motherhood was her only worthwhile role in life (along with taking care of her husband), and she internally accepted that belief as valid.

Today we live in a healthier social climate in which women can choose from many life-style options. But this availability of options where none existed previously can be a mixed blessing. Out of the wealth of options available to you, how do you know you are choosing the right one? In giving up past certainties that have proved unworkable, you also have to give up the certain comfort of having a major life decision made for you. For example, if you are a working mother who has freely chosen to resume your career three to six months after giving birth to your child, you may not be worried about what other people think of your decision (as women of your mother's generation would have been) because today, working and raising children no longer causes raised eyebrows. However, you yourself may be worried about whether or not you are doing the right thing for yourself and your family. This profound ambivalence is experienced by many other women who have made the same choice.

While you are at work, you may worry about the welfare of your child. But when you are home with your baby, you may feel that the time spent with him or her, enjoyable as it may be, "should" be spent advancing your career. After all, time is passing quickly, and you'd better maximize your efforts if you are going to rise on the career ladder. So while you are in your office, you feel a powerful pull to be with your baby, and while you are with your baby, you feel an equally powerful pull to pay attention to your career. In both instances you are liable to feel guilty about what you are doing at the moment. You like your job, you love your child, and you want to maximize the potentialities inherent in both to make your life a happy one. You may, in fact, be very much surprised that you are feeling such conflict. Before you had your baby, you might have felt sure that you could handle your career and a child at the same time without conflict. Oh, sure, you thought, it might involve minor inconveniences: some juggling of schedules, some additional effort to arrange proper child care, and some cooperation from your husband, who agreed to give it. But what seemed reasonble in theory turned into guilt-provoking ambivalence in practice.

The feeling seeps through you that maybe you chose the wrong route in life, when once you were so confident it was the right one. You have no answer for "Where did I go wrong?" because you wanted to experience the delights of both mothering and career.

This dilemma can be solved constructively, because your need to nurture yourself in your career and your need to nurture your child are not in competition at all. Both needs are part of your development, the full range of which can only emerge through an entire lifetime. In your earlier years, your need to develop your career self was the top priority in your life. But once your career started to become established, another need emerged: the need to develop the nurturing-mother part of yourself. Both needs should be welcomed, for each is entitled to fulfillment.

So why the internal conflict? The answer lies in recognizing that the conflict is misplaced and misdirected. It is caused by society, not by your inner needs. Society creates this contradiction by not providing affordable, high-quality, professional child care. The conflict is also created by corporations that do not allow for part-time and flexible-time working arrangements or for breaks in schedules when a working mother has to tend to an emergency. Small wonder that there seems to be a contradiction, when working mothers must worry constantly about both the security of their jobs and the welfare of their children.

When you recognize that the conflict is societally created, you can channel your energy outward and join organizations working for constructive solutions instead of flagellating yourself for being a "bad" mother or an "inadequate" worker or professional.

7. **The challenge to prevent the power of your upbringing to subvert your best intentions to become an equal partner and modern parent.**

With the birth of a child, you become instant "mother" and "father." What we know about these words derives largely from what we observed of our own parents' behavior while we were growing up. That imprinting can prove to be far more potent in influencing our behavior toward our own children than all the sensible books on modern parenting we may ever read.

In our practice, we recently worked with a two-career family couple who vividly exemplified this fact. Justin and Kendal are in their early thirties, and Arnold is their two-year-old son. Before Arnold was born, they both worked and shared the household chores. They prided themselves on being an enlightened couple. Justin was involved in all stages of the pregnancy and was pleased to be the coach at his son's birth. He even cut the umbilical cord. Kendal returned to her job as office manager after a nine-month leave of absence. She was astounded at the change in Justin after Arnold's birth. Let Kendal relate how she manages:

"After I got up at 5:00 A.M. to take a shower, I would take care of our little boy and make breakfast for Justin and myself. Then I would pick up all of Arnold's stuff to take to the baby-sitter with him. I would leave at 7:15 to get to the baby-sitter and then get to work by 8:10. During my lunch hour I would grab a bite and spend most of my time going to the cleaners or grocery shopping, because you're always out of something, like bread or milk. I'd get home at a quarter to six, after picking up Arnold from my baby-sitter. Justin would be home by 6:30, and maybe I would be able to catch up with the breakfast dishes and start dinner. Then I'd have to go right back to dealing with Arnold. After I finished cleaning up, I would only have an hour to spend with my baby, because he'd go to bed by 8:00.

"Justin changed completely once we brought the baby home from the hospital. He expected me to make his breakfast and his brown-bag lunch and have his dinner on the table when he got home. His idea of helping was clearing the dishes off the table. He would take the dishes from the dining room table to the kitchen, a distance of six feet. After exhausting himself with that hard work, he would sit back and watch TV or read his newspaper while I played with the baby and put him to sleep. I'd go to bed exhausted around 9:30 or 10:00, and then wake up every three or four hours to tend to the baby. Justin would never get out of bed; he'd say, 'That's your job,' when the baby woke us up in the middle of the night. I got tired of yelling at Justin to help me. I suppose an even bigger surprise for me than Justin's weird attitude was that I only got to see my baby two hours each day—just before going to work, and just after dinner. If Justin doesn't change, I'm going to leave him. He's like another kid around the house that I have to take care of, not my husband. Where did the Justin I love disappear to?"

Justin and Kendal came to us to find the answer to that question. When we explored with Justin the ways in which his father had acted while he was growing up and how his father had behaved when Justin's brother, who is three years younger, was born, the puzzle was solved. "Dad let Mom do all the work," Justin recalled. "He was the only one who brought a paycheck home and felt he had done enough for the family by 'breaking his ass all day,' as he used to say, working as an advertising salesman. Whatever happened at home was 'woman's work,' according to him, so he felt entitled to do nothing but relax after he got home. It's a funny thing, I've never gotten to really know my Dad. I still remember him—he's been dead ten years—sitting in front of the TV with a bottle of beer when I was dying to talk to him but afraid to interrupt him."

What Justin was describing was a carbon copy of his own behavior. When we brought this to his attention, he exclaimed, "My God, I became my father, something I vowed I would never do to my own wife and child!" He had thought Kendal was just being crabby and unfair when she observed how he had changed after Arnold's birth, but now he saw the accuracy of her criticisms. Now that he was aware that he had unconsciously replicated his father's behavior as a husband and parent, he was able to eliminate that behavior, and became the involved, nurturing father and equal-sharing spouse he had always determined to be.

Fortunately today when couples find themselves engaging in negative turnaround behavior like Justin's when they become parents, they increasingly seek out marriage counseling, rather than letting it destroy the relationship.

**8. The challenge to reconsider the possibility of becoming late parents.**

As recently as a decade ago, choosing to become a first-time parent after the age of thirty-five was considered chancy and exceptional and fraught with the danger of either miscarriage or some kind of disability. It has now been medically documented that the dangers were highly overrated. Normal births after thirty-five are the rule rather than the exception, and tests such as amniocentesis monitor the possibility of difficulties. Therefore, first-time parenthood at thirty-five or forty is now a rapidly growing, socially acceptable life-style option.

Many couples, however, still hesitate to choose this option, even though they know that the physical risks of birth are only slightly higher than for younger couples. Usually, it's because a husband and wife disagree about wanting a child. It is the biological difference between men and women that usually triggers such a disagreement. Because women's childbearing opportunities will end before their mid-forties, biology itself forces them into a last-chance decision whether or not to have a child. It matters little that the wife may have said, in her twenties or early thirties, that she would "never" have a child, or that she and her husband may have made an agreement to that effect. Now that she is older and must make a decision that will fundamentally affect the rest of her life, she may change her mind. On the other hand, a husband has no biological pressure of this kind—he can be fertile until the end of his life.

Biology isn't the only factor for women making a decision about parenthood. The psychological urge to experience childbearing and rearing is equally strong. When a husband doesn't understand these new realities in his wife's life, he may feel puzzled, hurt, and "betrayed," and then angrily say things to her like, "You always said you never wanted to have children, and now you've gone back on your word. You don't see me going back on my word."

When husband and wife experience a clash of attitudes like this, the marriage can be placed in grave jeopardy if the issue of having a child isn't mutually resolved without resentment and hurt feelings. When there is enough love left in a relationship, a couple can overcome their differences and surprise themselves with the delight of having a child late in life.

This is what happened to a couple we worked with who were on the brink of divorce over this issue. Their story is an encouraging example of what can happen when a husband and wife love each other enough to agree to have a child without one partner feeling intimidated into changing his or her mind.

Robert is now forty-eight, Jennifer is forty-three, and Elizabeth is three. But seven years ago the very idea that Robert and Jennifer would start a family would have seemed impossible to them. Things had changed when Jennifer turned thirty-six, and the idea of having a child began to really appeal to her; Robert's viewpoint was exactly the opposite, as it had always been.

"It surprised me," Jennifer said, "to discover that my biological clock told me to pay attention to it when I became thirty-six. You see, I wasn't really sure I wanted to have any children before Robert and I married. We did talk about the possibility, but Robert was not too happy with the idea, so we decided to postpone further talk about it until after we married. However, we never really talked about it during our first five years of marriage. There didn't seem to be any need to. We loved each other very much and were so happy doing things together.

"My early experience in life with children wasn't a happy one. I was the oldest of five in my family and had to take care of my two brothers and two sisters all the time. I felt I had done all the work of motherhood with none of the rewards. My brothers and sisters didn't appreciate my watching them, and my parents just took it for granted that because I was the oldest it was my obligation. If anything, I would say my tendency was to think that I probably would not have a child of my own, nor would I miss having one. So when the urge came over me at thirty-six to think about really having my own child, it was with mixed feelings. It hit me when I saw other friends at my age having a first child that I really would have to make a decision before it was too late—by the time I was forty. For four more years I grappled with my own mixed feelings before I felt 100 percent sure I wanted a child more than anything else in my life."

Robert told us that initially, for him, talk about having a baby was strictly a nonissue. "Like, yeah, we'll talk about it some day, blah, blah," he said. "During those four years, I was not on her wavelength at all. As I saw it, we had a very busy and fulfilling life as a couple, and I couldn't see how a child would fit into it. I was very certain I didn't want to be an absent father,

like my own father. I would want to be an active part of the
parenting process if we had a child. But I couldn't see that happening. We had a good standard of living to maintain, and a
child would force me to work even harder, so I couldn't be anything else but an absent father. I also resented the notion that
Jennifer would have the time to enjoy the child, while all I could
be doing was worrying about the bills. She'd have all the freedom while I would only have all the work.

"There was a point where we were real stuck, when I was
clear I didn't want a child and Jennifer was equally clear she
did. I saw it more as a limiting thing—a kid would limit the
things I most like to do, like traveling and being a fishing nut.
And I didn't want to share Jennifer. I thought I would lose a lot
of my freedom and my wife, too."

Jennifer then said, "I started to feel we needed something
more in our relationship and I needed something more in my
life. I wanted the opportunity to be selfless, to get out of my
own way and be totally present for another human being. It was
a different feeling from the way I felt as a 'little mother' to my
brothers and sisters. I had resented that because it was not my
choice; it was thrust upon me. But having my own child would
be my free choice: I wanted a deeper commitment. I felt in my
heart of hearts that more of me would be available to Robert,
rather than less."

Both Robert and Jennifer told us that this antagonism had
reached a point where both of them were seriously thinking
about divorce. The issue had to be decided without one feeling
intimidated by the other. They agreed that if they decided to
have a child, it would have to be a decision based on free choice.

Jennifer said the answer to their dilemma came when she
became absolutely certain that she wanted a child. "It all crys-
tallized for me one night when we were in bed after discussing
what our goals would be for the next year. I kept thinking about

it, and all I could come up with was 'I have only one goal: a child.' Over and over and over again that was the only answer. For the first time, it was unconditional—nothing else mattered but having a child. And I wanted that child with the only man I loved—Robert. Tears came to my eyes as I looked at Robert and said, 'You tell me what I have to do to have a child with you, and I'll do it. I want a child with no one else but you, and I'm making no demands other than that.'

"I wasn't willing until that moment to give up my standard of living, the nice trips, the nice house, and working part time. Robert was right. Until then I wanted it all—to have the freedom while he did all the work. I wasn't willing to give up anything until that moment when I knew beyond a shadow of a doubt that I really wanted a family above all else. Then my values got clear. I realized I didn't care about the rest of it—all I wanted was a child, a family, with this man, with Robert, and if it meant a lower standard of living, selling our house and moving to another state, or his staying home to experience nurturing our child while I worked, so be it."

Robert told us, "It was like a door opening. I knew then, for the very first time, that we weren't locked into stereotyped roles and the need to maintain a fairly expensive life-style to the exclusion of everything else once we had a child. We could really be a flexible team! All of a sudden all kinds of possibilities opened up for me. I could do anything, even staying home to take care of the kid while she went to work."

Jennifer made her decision out of absolute certainty and a sense of power within herself, not out of fear and desperation. Robert realized this and said, "Once she freed me from the stereotype of what a good father should be like, it shifted our discussions from 'whether or not to have a child' to 'how' we would do it. My decision to have a child became as unconditional as Jennifer's—it really was a free choice on my part too."

The fact that both Jennifer and Robert are in the second half of their lives has made them more perceptive and involved with their child than they would have been in their more pressured younger years. They have a longer view, a more relaxed sense of themselves. Older first-time parents are not aware of how very valuable these mature traits are until their child arrives, when they can then put their insights into practice.

What is the downside of becoming a late parent?

Robert quickly responded, "I'll be sixty when Elizabeth is fifteen, and when she's in college I'll be sixty-five. She's going o have to do some things on her own, and that's okay. I'm much more concerned about my physical condition now, because I want to be around as long as possible. If I die, it would be an incalculable loss to Elizabeth. So that starts to weigh in and make me shy away from the high-risk things I used to enjoy doing. I used to drive like a maniac and take chances on a motorcycle. No more. I don't wade quite as deep when I go fishing. I'm just a little less likely to stick my neck out."

Jennifer's immediate response to this question was a feeling of regret. "When Elizabeth is forty, I'll probably be dead, or very old. I'm sad about that. I wish we had gotten off the dime ten years earlier. I would have liked to have more years with her—and have grandchildren. We have less time than younger parents have. And I wonder, Is she going to be ashamed of us because we will be so much older than other parents?"

Robert quickly intervened at this point and said, "There are many more people like us having children in their forties. I don't think Elizabeth will believe we will be that different from other parents when she gets older."

We asked, If they had it to do all over again, would they still become parents?

They responded almost in unison: "It's impossible for us to think for one moment of a lifetime without Elizabeth!"

Of course, there are trade-offs for choosing to have a child late in life rather than in one's twenties or thirties. Awareness of the preciousness of time enables older first-time parents to place greater emphasis on the quality of the time spent with their child, time that younger parents are more liable to squander than to use constructively. The answer to the question, When is the right time to have children? is that there is no right time. There are only right people, people who are ready to care, love, validate, nurture, and enjoy their children; people who welcome their children into this world as a celebration of a marriage that is happy to start with, but will be happier still with a child.

9. **The challenge to consider adoption as a happy alternative to living a childless life because of infertility.**

Today, adoption is no longer considered a "second-best" solution. Society has validated adoption as an alternative choice that can be as vitalizing and enriching to a relationship as a biological child would be. And psychological findings confirm that an adopted child can flourish in the love and nurturing of adoptive parents. This is true not only of adoption by heterosexual couples but also of adoption by single mothers or fathers or lesbian or gay domestic partners.

We would like to share with you the adoption experience of a couple we worked with. Their insights will prove helpful to those who despair over their infertility, to those who are ambivalent about adopting, or to those who have made the decision to adopt but don't know what their next steps should be:

Sally and Cary are both forty-one and jointly operate a successful designer clothing business. Eleven months ago they adopted Daniel at birth, but the road to that adoption was not a simple one. As Sally said, "Before we adopted Daniel we had been married ten years. The basic reason I didn't pursue with

Cary the idea of adoption until recently was because of an abortion I had when I was in my early twenties. I think that subconsciously my guilt over the abortion prevented me from conceiving my own child. And looking back now, I believe I made an unconscious promise to myself never to become pregnant again.

"Cary and I kept putting off having babies because we had a business to build. There was always some reason—or some excuse—that everything else came first before having children. Then when we finally decided to do it I discovered I couldn't conceive. I was thirty-six at that time. We tried everything, but nothing worked. I really wanted a child, but something inside me was holding me back. I would have a false pregnancy every month at the time I had my period. My breasts would get sore, my stomach would bloat. I would take many pregnancy tests, but I would screw up the tests so that it would look like I was pregnant. We finally gave up and later began to wonder about the alternative of adoption."

Cary joined in: "It was a race against age. We really always wanted to have children, but we never really stopped to make the time to do it. We tried to have our own child from the age of thirty-six to the age of forty. Then we finally decided to make time to have an adopted child. It wasn't just a matter of thinking about adopting; it was about doing it."

Sally agreed. "When we finally figured out it was a wash, that we couldn't have children, I first began to bury myself in work. We turned the business into a million-dollar company. Later, when I began seeing many of my friends, associates, and employees having babies, I would get sick to my stomach. Cary and I would talk about it. I realized I had a heartache and did not want to go through life without a child. We began to conclude that there wasn't anything we really wanted except a family. The longing for a child was always there like a cloud over our heads."

Cary said that at that time everything seemed hollow to them. "Socializing was hollow; holidays were empty. But when we ran across kids, we didn't feel empty. And we would say to ourselves, Wouldn't it be nice if we had children? It was then that we decided we could. There was an alternative, and that was to adopt."

Sally was frank to admit she was scared when they made the decision to definitely adopt. "I was so scared about whether I would make a good mother. You see, I had an alcoholic mother and a workaholic father, so there wasn't much closeness in my family. My fear was that I would be like Mom, that I would replicate my own painful family situation."

Sally's fear did not prevent them from pursuing adoption. When you are ready for an important new stage in your life, the universe sometimes gives you a positive push in the right direction. That happened to Cary and Sally one night at dinner:

"We saw a couple in the restaurant sitting near us who had two children with them. I was smiling at the children, and I said to Cary, 'Why can't that be us?' After they finished dinner, the couple turned to us and asked, 'Do you have children?' I said, 'No, but we are considering adopting.' They then told us the children with them were adopted. They joined us with their children and gave us the name of an attorney who specialized in adoptions.

"On our way to see the attorney, we were so nervous. We looked at each other and said, 'Are we dressed like parents? Do we look like parents?' Our experience with the attorney was disappointing, but it turned out it was a good learning experience for us. Now I know if you don't feel good with a lawyer, leave and choose another. Because you go on a roller coaster ride in adoption, you need the help of a lawyer who is a moral human being, someone you can call in the middle of the night if need be. If an attorney tells you that you're on the clock when you are calling him, if he doesn't write down any of your questions, stay away from him. Our new attorney loves what he does, and he's now a friend.

"I got three calls from mothers through our second attorney. He asked me if I would consider taking a baby 'on call.' That means that sometimes mothers after they have given birth to their babies, or right before, decide to give them up for adoption. I told him, yes we would. I got a call from a mother four hundred miles away who had decided to give up her baby at the last moment, so Cary and I flew down to meet her.

"The baby was adorable, and I picked up the baby and held her and fell in love with her. Our lawyer had said to speak to the obstetrician and also my pediatrician to make sure everything was okay. But everything was not okay. The baby I had fallen in love with had urine that showed cocaine. My pediatrician and lawyer both told me not to accept the child and to leave the hospital at once. I cried and cried. I had fallen so in love with her."

Cary said this traumatic experience was really positive for Sally and him. It showed how much they really wanted a baby. "If we could go through an incident like that, we certainly had the strength to adopt," he said.

With their lawyer's guidance, they continued the effort to adopt, and one month later they were able to start the process of adopting Daniel.

Sally said, "After the ordeal with a cocaine-addicted birth mother, I decided that when we adopted I would want personal contact with the birth mother—to check her out down to her toenails—her life-style, her physical condition, her behavior. So when Martin called us again, he arranged for us to meet a new mother-to-be in his office. I knew immediately she was the one. We embraced each other, and I knew in that instant that baby was going to be mine.

"I believe it's really important to pay attention to your own feelings when you are meeting the prospective mother-to-be. The adoptive mother has to feel this is right; this feels good; this is my baby. And the birth mother has to feel with the adoptive mother that this is the right place for her baby to be.

"We were there for the birth of the baby. The obstetrician placed the baby in my arms. Cary cut the cord. We knew we were going to call him Daniel, and he looked right up to me, and he's been with me ever since."

Daniel was a healthy, alert, and active baby. However, neither Cary or Sally felt entirely secure that they would be able to keep him. Six months later, the adoption was legally finalized. (In their state there is a waiting period of six months during which a birth mother can change her mind and legally demand the return of the child.)

Sally recalls that "for six months I was so scared that the birth mother would come and take Daniel back. The possibility that someone could take him from me during the six months was so frightening that I held back a little, just a little, until the finalizing. I wouldn't leave him for a moment; I felt so afraid I would lose him.

"On the day we went to court, our lawyer was with us. And as we got into the hallway where the courtroom was, I looked up and down the hallway, looking for the birth mother to take the baby from me. I looked for her in the courtroom also, and then I started crying, because that was the last look. The doors of the courtroom were closed, and I was safe.

"After Daniel became ours legally, I was more relaxed about Cary and me being Daniel's parents."

Sally and Cary have found a great sense of personal self-renewal and greater closeness as a couple now that Daniel has permanently entered their lives. We asked them if their priorities in life have changed since they adopted Daniel. Here are their answers:

Sally: "My priorities are terribly different. I've been a working woman all my life, creating and running companies. But with Daniel, I did not go to the office for six months, and I didn't give a damn. Instead of going to the office in great deliberation and spending all day and into the night thinking about the company, I now get it done in about an hour and a half, by phone from home. My family comes first. I think I will lead a much better life because of adopting Daniel. Everything has a new perspective. You are watching this little new person react to the world, and all of a sudden things aren't quite as heavy; there is a new brightness to the world.

"Daniel's coming into our lives was a completion for me. In that regard, I think Cary has had a better woman to deal with, because Daniel is making me feel complete as a woman, a full human being. I never saw this adoption as a solution but as an addition to our lives."

Cary: "Daniel has shifted our priorities. I always wanted to come home and have a child there to greet me. As I get up at night and walk in his room, his delighted little face looking up at me makes things look new for me. I expected to show Daniel the world, but so far he has shown the newness of the world to me.

"The decision to have Daniel in my life allows me to interact with a lot of people. Another thing, you walk around and see other children, and you realize, My gosh, I've been walking around for twenty-some years, and I have never noticed the joy in other children. I get to see the joy in other children through Daniel.

Rather than having our business as our surrogate child, Daniel is our *real* child. We don't have to search out all these other things to make us happy, because Daniel, without the fuss, makes us happy. Sally and I have been married for ten years and our company operated as our surrogate child. We treated the company as a family that one day would be all grown up and healthy and happy. We were treating business employees and our clients as if they were part of our family. We learned our company is *not* our family. For the first time in ten years I come home and we don't talk about the business. Instead we talk about what the three of us can do together as a family. I think it's funny when we take Daniel to our business; we smile, thinking there's no way this business is our child!

"Daniel is a part of our lives; he's not in the way of it. Sally and I love each other—and he feels that, I'm sure."

We asked Cary and Sally what they felt about telling Daniel he was adopted. Cary said, "It's all right to tell him early, when he's three or four or around that time. A second cousin of mine didn't know he was adopted until he was eighteen. It blew him apart and he's been angry at his adoptive parents ever since."

Sally agreed with Cary. "I wrote Daniel a poem, which I'll give him when we tell him he was adopted," she said. When we read the poem we were so touched by its truth and poignancy that we asked her permission to share it with our readers. She gave us that permission.The questions in the poem are the kind of questions an adopted child needs answers to. The response to these questions are the deeply felt answers Sally will give to Daniel:

"Mommy, what does it mean to be adopted?"

I think what you are asking me is, Did you come from inside me?
Yes, my darling son,
You came from every dream that Mommy ever dreamed
And you came from the deepest hope that I have ever

held in my heart,
And you came from my every prayer that God heard,
And you came from every silent whisper, waiting for you
to arrive.

"But Mommy, am I yours?"

My darling, you are more mine than I am to myself,
You are the answer that God heard,
You are the love that I had waited for
And before you I had not understood.
Are you ours? You belong to God, my angel, not to me
As every child you know belongs to God.
You are his creation alone
And the world has been blessed by your smile.

"Mommy, is there a tummy I came from?"

Yes, dear son, you came from a tummy.
I will bring her to meet you one day,
The woman whose tummy you come from loved you
so very much.
She knew that God wanted you with Daddy and me.
She was the vessel of life that brought you to us.
All of us belong to each other, my child,
We are on earth to love and to share
And to give love to one another.
Whether you came from my tummy or someone else's
You are my dear son whom God blessed for my keeping.
You will live your life in love and grace
And you will have an understanding of universal love
Because of the way you came to this world.
So, my dearest, you asked me, "What does it mean

to be adopted?"
What do you think it means?

"Mommy, I think that I came here to love and to be loved
It isn't the tummy I came from: It's the way I feel.
Goodnight, Mommy."

## 10. The challenge to become a good-enough parent.

We have called this third marriage of your marriage the good-enough-parent marriage to emphasize that there is no such thing as a perfect parent. Because children are uniquely themselves as well as products of both a mother and a father, they will continually surprise us. A "perfect" parent would have children whose behavior is 100 percent predictable. But the only way such predictability could be achieved would be to give birth to a programmed robot.

Our objective in this chapter is to free parents from feeling guilty for not being "perfect" parents. Because it is the rare parent who doesn't love his or her children and want the best for them, it's natural to have a persistent feeling that best is not good enough. Speaking as parents ourselves, we experienced this concern as our own children were growing up. However, it is one thing to have a nurturing concern about doing the best we can for our children. It is quite another to translate that concern into feeling unrealistically guilty about not being perfect parents.

The greatest manufacturer of this guilt trip on parents is society itself. The advertising media plant the virus of guilt in every parent whose children say, "I want what I've just seen on TV." The ads suggest that you can rid yourself of "guilt" by buying the various commodities they pitch. The trend among government officials and politicians is to proclaim the virtues of family life and parenthood. It's like being against sin; who could protest that? But these same representatives, who feel free to tell parents to become "more perfect," are curiously silent about their own neglect of family issues. When our government refuses to take even the first steps to improve the quality of our decaying schools or to adopt a national policy of paid maternity and paternity leave like the ones every other responsible industrial country has, when it ignores the crying need for a network of inexpensive high-quality child-care centers and won't affirm the need for flex-time and part-time work schedules to prevent child neglect, it seems more than arrogant for government officials to place the blame on parents for being less than perfect. How can a parent be expected to be perfect when 37 million Americans can't afford health insurance or decent health care, and the government does nothing about it?

Though none of us can become perfect parents, we can all become good-enough parents by differentiating between unrealistic and realistic parental guilt. Unrealistic guilt comes out of buying society's definition of a "perfect" parent and finding you don't measure up to it. As we've just outlined, the real guilty parties are societal institutions like advertising agencies, television, and government.

To be realistically guilty means that parents need to get involved in political action to elect representatives and a president who will be responsive to the needs of our children and institute the programs we have noted above. It is certainly our responsibility to involve ourselves in improving our schools and giving more quality time to our children. Were our government indeed improving our schools and legislating changes to our work arrangements and we did not take advantage of those changes, we would be guilty.

Parents can free themselves from unrealistic guilt by refusing to succumb to their children's endless demands for the latest products. They will thereby teach their children that there are alternative ways of making oneself happy, by creating things and doing things instead of buying them.

Unrealistic guilt is also at the heart of the lack of parental guidance and excessive permissiveness. When both parents work all day and feel that in doing so they've neglected their children, their "guilt" may take the form of allowing their children to run roughshod over other people. Notice, for example, how many children in restaurants are allowed by their parents to shout, shove, run around, and ignore the sensitivities of the other people who are eating. It's not because the parents are insensitive to what is happening; it's because they feel guilty about the limited time they spend with their children and therefore feel it's not right to deprive their children of their little pleasures. What this behavior teaches children, however, is that insensitive self-indulgence is perfectly appropriate. To be a responsible parent means teaching your children to be sensitive to other people's needs and to understand that setting limits to their behavior is a sign of parental love. Setting limits will also give them a sense of personal security.

The good-enough parent is a parent who recognizes his or her limitations. We are deluding ourselves if we believe our children can be models of our expectations rather than their own. We can teach them to be personally responsible for their behavior, so that they will feel accountable to themselves first of all. We can show them that they are loved by their parents, that they are loved for who they are rather than what they do. We can set responsible limits for them and discipline them if they violate those limits. This can be educational rather than punitive.

But the strongest messages we can send to our children are through our own behavior, through seeing that their parents love each other and live in a violence-free, drug-free house. It is that secure, stabilized love that will provide children with the sense of inner security they'll need to guide themselves through the world.

Of course, the parent-child connection continues in one form or another until the day you die. But it is in those infant, toddler, and preschool years that you put most of your energy and concentration into defining who you are as a mother and a father. Your survival as a couple and as working people continue to be important during the good-enough-parent marriage, but stabilization of your new roles as parents takes top priority. Once that occurs, the time-is-running-out marriage begins to happen.

*Chapter Six*

# The Time-Is-Running-Out Marriage

For most marriages, when partners are somewhere in their forties, the children are in school, and some may even be thinking about leaving home for college. If you were born in the baby-boom generation (and you probably were, because two-thirds of our population are baby boomers), you were told constantly by the media that you were the golden children—that you would be eternally prosperous, healthy, and young. But they lied: now you look in the mirror and see the wrinkles that have stamped their imprint on your forehead, eyes, or neck, or the gray hairs and receding hairline that weren't there yesterday, or the paunch that can no longer be rationalized out of existence. You find that your children have become adolescents!

You've lived through so many of their developmental stages —the demanding infant, the assertive toddler, the seductive pre-schooler, the tractable schoolboy or schoolgirl, and now this! And just as your children shed those earlier stages of physical and psychological development, so will this turbulent adolescence end. Your children, in a flick of a few years, will become adults. Yet it seems like only yesterday they were cradled in your arms or proudly wheeled in their carriages.

This is the time in life when people you know die—not notables headlined in newspapers, but acquaintances, friends, and relatives. A friend in his thirties may die of a heart attack or AIDS, an aunt or uncle of leukemia, a parent of a stroke; adolescent friends of your children die of drug overdoses or in car accidents; a work acquaintance succumbs from alcoholism; the couple down the block may split up and the husband turns a gun on himself. Events like these are reminders that the bell tolls for everyone and that it's time to make the most of your finite time in this world.

Men frequently get depressed in their mid-thirties. If they haven't "made it" by then, they try to turn back the clock by having affairs or getting divorced. This is still known as "the seven-year itch" and used to be reserved for men. Today more and more women are getting it too. And if a husband and wife somehow survived that early confrontation with age, they may very well experience the "fifteen-year itch" in their forties. Over one-fourth of all divorces occur in marriages of fifteen years' duration or longer.

Moving toward middle age can have an especially traumatic impact on women, for this is an age-haunted society that tells us that youth is "good" and growing older is "bad," particularly for women. Despite all the recent talk about the attractiveness of older women, most women are still captives of the belief that the image of youth is the only one that counts. A wife may look at herself and her husband and find both wanting. She may be tempted to try to recapture her youth via exercise, weight reduction, trendy clothes, or a bit of plastic surgery around the eyes or mouth. This desperate search for the fountain of youth ensnares men, too. This is the time when men dye their hair, seek out plastic surgeons, diet and exercise, and don new wardrobes. But this frenetic "victory" over age is a hollow triumph if it means growing older fearfully rather than gracefully.

Couples who find themselves in the time-is-running-out marriage will discover a proliferation of new triangle entrapments and the challenges to overcome them. This is unexplored territory. How the two of you travel through it will determine the measure of your future closeness as a couple.

## *The Typical Marriage Triangles in the Time-Is-Running-Out Marriage*

### *The Two-Can-Be-Lonelier-Than-One Sexual Triangle*

In the late thirties a curious thing happens on the way to the bedroom. A woman finds she is becoming more sexual and sensual, while her husband might feel less and less sexually able. As the children grow older, a wife may feel, "Now is the time for me." The nurturing part of her fulfilled, she may be more in touch with her own needs as a vital, orgasmic woman.

On the other hand, the strain and tension, worry and fear her husband has experienced in trying to climb the ladder of business success might have taken a psychological toll that negatively affects his sexual desire and performance.

Sexual estrangement can become the daily pattern of a couple's life if this situation is not resolved constructively. By the time they are in their forties, a wife may convince herself that sex with her husband is little more than an occasional assault with a dead weapon. And her husband may begin to believe that good sex is available to every man in this world but him. In many such marriages, masturbation takes the place of lovemaking. Separate bedrooms and a silent mutual pact not to have any sex at all is a frequent "solution." A wife in this situation has long given up sending out signals that she is eager for lovemaking. A distracted good-bye peck on the mouth or cheek as he leaves for work and one when he returns home is the sum total of his sexual activity.

Should their discontent develop into chronic avoidance of any sharing of their feelings that something is going seriously wrong between them, a two-can-be-lonelier-than-one sexual triangle will emerge. And if that triangle persists, it will become a measure of the deterioration of their marriage.

## The Anyone-But-My-Spouse Triangle

The conviction that you are no longer your spouse's number one can undergo intense reinforcement at this time. The anyone-but-my-spouse triangle begins with the feeling that your spouse is always putting you down, is inconsiderate and unappreciative of all your efforts to make home a happy place. And besides, he or she is boring, boring, boring! Surely there's someone else "out there" who will appreciate you for who you are. You're fortyish, but look younger; you're still attractive and intelligent. In contrast to your present spouse, who may be a sexual desert, your dream person is a sexual oasis. Oh, not a divorce, you justify, but an exciting affair to liven up your marriage. And these thoughts seem to be validated when a husband reads that 60 percent of all married men in the United States have had affairs; a wife reads the same surveys and discovers that an almost equal number of married women have had at least one affair. If the desire is strong enough, these thoughts can become reality. But instead of bringing rejuvenation, the typical affair is a guilt-ridden, what-if-I-get-a-sexually-transmitted-disease, when-will-I-be-found-out?, anxiety-provoking experience. The sex may be more exciting, but its price in terms of the loss of marital trust and loyalty is very high. These values may turn out to be much more important to you than you once thought.

## The Making-Up-for-Lost-Time Triangle

There is another triangle in which the third party in your relationship is not an individual but the panic in your mind. The making-up-for-lost-time triangle occurs in response to intensification of the feeling that time is running out and there may never be a tomorrow. An accumulation of factors can trigger this response: the death of a friend, your own aging, the suddenly deep voice and manly height of your son or the daughter who is now a curvaceous young woman. If nothing is certain, self-centered indulgence may seem like an attractive solution. The consequences need not be considered, because you have only one life to live, and it's a short one. So you try what you've never tried: drugs, boisterous partying, "swinging" with like-minded couples, a new wardrobe fit for a twenty-year-old, a sports car, an abrupt separation from your spouse, separate vacations that are really searches for affairs. But all this frantic activity by a husband or wife or both is fueled by fear and despair. Instead of making up for lost time, the activity itself becomes lost time.

## The Shattered-Dreams Triangle

The third party in the shattered-dreams triangle is your own feelings of regret. A self-pitying, continuous concern about what might have been, rather than what can constructively be done now, takes possession of your mind. There is the shattered dream of the perfect mate. You thought you married that ideal person, and now you find yourself thinking that if you had it to do all over again, you wouldn't have chosen your spouse. And with this thought comes regret over the oh-so-many "better" marriage choices (all more attractive and now much more successful than your spouse) that you foolishly turned down.

There is the shattered dream of being the perfect parent. Here you are, saddled with children whose behavior, ideas, and values clash with your own. Regret pierces your soul: "If I had a second chance, I could do better next time." There is the shattered dream of great professional success. That big house, that top job, that fat bank account, and that applause for your accomplishments are still dreams when they should be realities. Regret takes the place of material success. Sadness over lost opportunities fuses with poignant feelings that it should have been otherwise. Regret in the form of uppers or downers or alcohol may become the number one "person" in your marriage.

## The My-Children-Love-Me-More-
## Than-You-Do Triangle

Overconcern and overinvolvement in your children's lives can become the third party in a triangle. As the years fly by and your children near adulthood, the parental bond requires loosening rather than tightening. If, however, you feel that you no longer count as number one with your spouse, you may seek the love you need elsewhere in the family. The children become the target of all the love you want to give and the love you are not receiving from your spouse.

In this situation, parental love gets confused with adult marital love. You have already experienced parental love toward your children, but now emotional deprivation may become so intense that you unconsciously try to solicit adult love from them, too. You then send out double signals to your children that say in effect, "Love me as a parent, but also love me as an adult." In extreme cases, a husband or wife may act out this need for adult love by making their children the recipient of irrational, incestuous attention. (We now know that incest is far more widespread than it was once assumed to be.) More typical, however, are the instances in which a father notices that his daughter is turning into an attractive adult. He may be surprised, embarrassed, and shocked over his burgeoning sexual feelings toward her. Or he may start fondling her, embracing her, kissing her excessively in ways that resemble a lover's more than a parent's. Or a wife may start calling her son "my handsome young man" and showering him with intense kisses, which makes him very uncomfortable. In lieu of her own husband, he becomes her "escort"; she takes him on shopping sprees or visits to films or restaurants. The son becomes adept at making excuses to minimize her approaches.

These actions on the part of parents are not intentional. They arise from unfulfilled adult needs that are acted out in unaware ways. Paradoxically, these attempts at closeness alienate children; instead of receiving more love from them, parents receive less. Resentment, hostility, guilt, and fear are planted in children's psyches when inappropriate roles are imposed upon them.

There are other variations on this triangle: your overinvolvement with the children can take the form of becoming "just friends" with them. You convince yourself that you're "one of the boys" or "one of the girls." The language you use may take on the coloration of the "in" words your children speak. You may not think you are acting seductively or competitively with your adolescent daughter's or son's friends when they visit, but your children are annoyed and embarrassed by your one-of-the-gang overfriendliness. The Little League sports or high school games your children participate in become your games, and your kids start to feel it's not really their game anymore but yours. They get the impression they are loved by you only if they win. The closeness you want from them turns into its opposite.

## The Real-Estate Triangle

Your home or the dream house that exists in a corner of your mind becomes the seducer in the real estate triangle. This can happen when you feel your own sense of self-worth deteriorating. If your spouse is not validating your personal worth, you may seek that validation from something stable and permanent, such as your house. Property represents permanence and stability, values that seem more important than before, now that everything seems to be slipping away. You shift your energies from your relationship with your spouse to your relationship with your property. How your house is maintained becomes more important than your spouse, or you become passionately concerned about finding a new place. But wood, brick, stone, and land can never make you feel important to yourself. And your overconcern with your property can only widen the emotional gap between you and your spouse.

## The Rebellious-Teenager Triangle

With the advent of puberty, your teenage children have arrived. The qualities you used to proudly show off to friends and neighbors now appear to be nonexistent.

Mother and father know that there is a dangerous sexual world outside their front door. It's a fact that one-fourth of all fifteen-year-old girls have had sexual intercourse, and one million teenage girls get pregnant every year, resulting in 300,000 abortions. You can tell your daughter these facts and that each year 2.5 million teenagers are infected with sexually transmitted diseases, and you're then left to wonder how much these warnings sink in. Is our saintly daughter "doing it"? The worry is always present. And why is she so thin? Could her obsession with her figure make her anorexic or bulimic?

Though your son can't get pregnant, he can certainly be the partner of the girl who is (one-third of all fifteen-year-old boys have had sexual intercourse). He can become a problem drinker (two out of five high school children are binge drinkers); he can get involved with drugs; he can even attempt suicide (suicide is the second major cause of teenager deaths).

If there is no open line of communication between you as parents and your teenage children, a rebellious-teenager triangle will develop. As parents, you may become so overwhelmed with your children's real or imagined problems that each neglects nurturing the other as the number one person in his or her life.

## The Sandwich-Generation Triangle

As if dealing with your intractable teenagers weren't enough, you may find yourself contending with totally unexpected problems involving your aging parents. For as you move through this fourth marriage of your marriage, which ends by the time you reach fifty, your parents, now in their late sixties or seventies, may start to experience severe physical and psychological problems that demand your immediate attention. Because of our lengthening life spans (30 million Americans are sixty-five and older, and within two decades one in five persons will be in that age bracket; the fastest growing age category today is eighty-five years and older), more and more middle-aged couples will find themselves economically and physically supporting one or both of their ailing, aging sets of parents. Our society has already given a name to such middle-aged couples: the sandwich generation, that is, couples who are caught in the middle, still having to support their own dependent children and now their parents as well.

An aging parent may have a heart attack, terminal cancer, a stroke, or the beginning of Alzheimer's disease. He or she deserves your concern, physical presence, and economic support.

But they can also become fretful, fearful, anxiety-ridden, time-demanding, economic drains on your psyche and bank account. And as a consequence, you may feel guilt-ridden, resentful, or exhausted; you and your spouse may then experience "caretaker burnout," in which you both suffer the loss of your number one relationship with each other because the sandwich-generation triangle has taken its place.

## The Unexpected-Tragedy Triangle

Bad things can indeed happen to good people, and the time-is-running-out marriage is the period when many of them can begin to appear. There's the friend who never drank or smoked and ran four miles each morning who suddenly dies of a first heart attack or cancer at age forty-five, the death of your own parents, the car or motorcycle accident that puts your son or daughter in a wheelchair for life, your wife's breast cancer, your husband's triple-bypass operation, your son's or daughter's sudden suicide.

Why me? Anguish, resentment, fear, and hopelessness may overcome you as a couple. Tragedies of this nature can either bring a couple closer or estrange them forever. If you allow the unexpected-tragedy triangle to develop by focusing all of your energies on self-pity, guilt, hostility, regret, and resentment, the number one belief in each other will disappear.

## *Your Mutual Development Challenges*

In your time-is-running-out marriage, the man or woman within you is shouting to be heard. What you once took for granted about yourself is now a sea of uncertainty. Consequently, your new mutual development challenges evolve from the man or woman within you who is wondering, Who am I, and what do I want to do at this time in my life? This concern gives rise to the following key challenges:

1. **The challenge to come to terms with your own aging process.**

Are you encountering the older person you see in the mirror as a friend or as a vicious enemy? Do you feel the best part of your life is over, or that a different, but better, part of it is beginning? How you and your spouse respond to this challenge will determine the emotional climate in your household.

You still have half your life to live and may need to update your knowledge about aging. Modern scientific findings indicate that there's much you can do to keep yourself physically and mentally fit until the end of life. Your body and mind resemble an automobile: the more you use them and care for them, the greater their capabilities. Body and mind will deteriorate from nonuse or misuse, too, just as a car will.

## 2. The challenge to recondition your mind and your body.

Are the values you are attached to in need of reexamination? Does "success" mean big bucks in the bank and a top-of-the-heap job at the expense of everything else in life? Or does it mean accepting realistic limitations, letting go of an obsession with "making it," and paying primary attention to enriching your own life in nonmonetary ways, such as expanding your circle of friends, or taking that course in nutrition, painting, literature, music, or political science you always said you didn't have time for? Perhaps renewing your relationship with your spouse, getting to understand him or her better so that you can enjoy and love each other more is the best definition of "success" this world has to offer.

It may be time for you to pay renewed attention to your body as well as your mind. Excess fat, heart attacks, muscle deterioration, hypertension, and backaches are not necessary consequences of aging. How well you monitor and care for your body can often make the difference. An increase in awareness of the latest nutritional discoveries, a shift to a healthier diet and a program of reasonable exercise, and allowing yourself time to smell the flowers may do wonders for your physical condition.

## 3. The challenge to readjust your relationship with your children as they near adulthood.

Is your own identity so wrapped up in your role as parent that you cannot bear the thought of your children leaving home? Or are you so estranged from them that you can't wait until they leave? Do you treat your adolescent children as if they were still six or seven? Are you too permissive ("Why should I lay my trip on them?") or too controlling ("They are only kids, so I have to tell them what to do!")? Can you begin to treat your children more and more as adults as they near the end of their adolescence and at the same time maintain your role as a wise guide and reasonable limit-setter? How you respond to these questions will determine whether or not you can let go of your children lovingly or resentfully once they become adults and establish independent lives. They will continue to welcome you and regard you with love, respect, and affection once they leave home if you support their quest for independence while setting reasonable limits on their behavior.

Remember how you hated being lectured to and treated like a child by your father or mother long after you left home? Then catch yourself the next time you hear your own parents' voices in the way you talk to your adolescent sons and daughters and begin to treat them like the adults they are becoming.

### 4. The challenge to become authoritative parents who can deal skillfully with a teenager's out-of-control behavior.

This challenge arises when you readjust your relationship to your teenage children. To become an "authoritative" parent is to arm yourself with as much available knowledge as possible to help you respond skillfully to the difficult behavior your teenager may be exhibiting. This is quite the opposite of being an "authoritarian" parent—the kind of parent who demands blind submission to authority. The problem with this approach is that it doesn't work.

On the other hand, being an authoritative parent does work. Your children will listen to you because you have earned their respect by your empathy, understanding, and ability to educate them rather than dictate to them. Your influence is based on respect for your ability to help your children rather than on an arbitrary exercise of abusive power over them.

Of course, the first concern of any parent whose children are teenagers is how are they coping with their sexuality, for the hormones are indeed raging in both girls and boys at this stage in their lives. After all, at puberty they have developed their physical ability to reproduce sexually and are eager for sexual experimentation.

Because ours is a sex-drenched society, the authoritative parent knows that preventing a child from being interested in sex or from some degree of sexual activity is like trying to prevent the night from following the day. The objective, then, is to create a caring environment in which your teenager will feel free to ask you any question about sex he or she may be concerned about. Your children will not do so, however, if you're trying to answer with a lecture rather than with appropriate information. You may have to go to some effort to create an environment in which your teenager will want to talk freely to you about his or her sexual concerns, for it is still a sad fact that most teenagers are either afraid or embarrassed to talk openly and honestly with their parents about all of their feelings about sex. When they need knowledge, they usually solicit it from their peers, or from hearsay, or from TV. Needless to say, the information is frequently wrong or inadequate—all the more reason for you to be armed with knowledge that can be truly useful to your children, that counteracts the fantasy that may masquerade as fact. The Kinsey Institute *New Report on Sex* (New York: St. Martin's Press, 1990) has the most trustworthy factual information you will need for dialogues with your children.

Am I normal? is the basic question every teenager asks himself or herself. Your teenage daughter will probably worry over her breast size and when it's "normal" to begin menstruation, about whether it's "sinful" to masturbate.

Boys are primarily concerned about the size of their penises. "Are my testicles normal? Is my penis too small for intercourse?" When you reassure your child that he is well within the range of normalcy (the range for normalcy is wide indeed), you will enable your teenage son to feel comfortable as a sexual human being. That same reassurance is equally needed by your teenage daughter.

As an authoritative parent, you will be aware that teenage children will not tell you everything they and their peers are up to sexually. Even if their friends are out of line, they are protective of their behavior and don't want to see them punished. So if some of your children's peers drink alcohol to excess at parties, or do dope, or are into promiscuous intercourse with or without "protection," your children won't talk to you about it. But if you understand why, you can focus on their personal responsibility not to act that way. As an authoritative parent you will be educating your children to monitor themselves: to be protective of their own health and bodies, so that drugs or alcohol are used to a very limited degree, or not at all.

Most of all, you will be educating your children to think of sexual intercourse as a very special thing to be engaged in within a monogamous relationship, if at all, before marriage. There is no such thing as "safe" sex in these times; there is only "safer" sex. Despite all your wishes to the contrary, chances are your child will have intercourse before marriage. Professors Deborah A. Cohen and Erin A. Quinn of the Department of Family Medicine at the University of Southern California have some pertinent things to say on this question that you can share with your children:

> Magic Johnson's announcement that he is infected with HIV underscores the findings of researchers across the country that only modest changes in the sexual behavior

of Americans have occurred over the past decade. Unless a more aggressive approach to increasing the practice of safer sex is taken quickly, the AIDS epidemic may devastate America in the same manner as it has done in several African countries including Uganda, where one in five citizens in urban areas is infected. America's current social climate does not support or reinforce the consistent practice of safer sexual behavior. Even among those who have adopted safer sexual behavior, a considerable number relapse and engage in unprotected intercourse with casual sex partners. AIDS cases continue to increase among heterosexuals. The rate of infection in child-bearing women has increased by 40 percent in the past year. Teenage deliveries are up sharply, an indicator of the increase in unprotected teen-age sexual activity. In addition, there were 54,404 cases of gonorrhea and 10,457 cases of early syphilis in 1990, indicating continued widespread high-risk sexual behavior. Safer sex means intercourse while using a barrier contraceptive with no exchange of body fluids. Or it can mean intimate relations, such as hugging, massage and kissing, without intercourse. Latex condoms (rubbers) are the best method of protection for vaginal, anal or oral intercourse because they prevent contact with semen, cervical secretions and blood. . . .

Research has shown that people will use barrier contraceptives when they are familiar with them and have experience using them, in spite of all the drawbacks. One of the best ways to influence large numbers of people to change their behavior in a relatively short period of time is through social marketing—advertising whose goal is to promote public health. (*Los Angeles Times,* 10 November 1991)

Pat has this to say on the subject:

"Since they were tots, my two daughters, Karen and Vicky, would always feel free to tell me all their concerns, no matter what. If they wanted to close the door of their own rooms, play tapes, or even play with themselves, that was their affair. I always respected their privacy, since I was not going to scare them half to death the way my mother did me about masturbation. I did not want them in any way to feel self-conscious about their own bodies. I told them the facts about menstruation together—when Karen was twelve and Vicky eleven. I took the girls into the living room, turned off the lights, and lit a candle around which we sat on the floor. When I informed them about the physiological change they would soon undergo, the soft, dim candlelight enabled them to question me more freely without exposing them to any embarrassment.

"When I told them about sexual intercourse some time later, it turned out to be a waste of time. I asked them, "What do you know or what have you heard from your friends about where babies come from?" Their answers blew my mind. They knew almost as much as I did! What they didn't know was anything about contraceptives. Oh yes, they had heard about the pill, but they were surprised at the wide variety of different kinds of contraceptives that I proceeded to tell them about.

"More than anything else, I tried to impress upon them the fact that the sexual act was a demonstration of love or real caring for a person. It was not something to be lightly indulged in, if at all, prior to marriage. A temporary infatuation with a boy was no reason for going to bed with him. Enjoying his company should be enough. Set limits for yourself, I told them, and if a boy didn't respect those limits, he would make you unhappy later on. I made a remark that they could get a bellyache from treating sex as if it were a box of candy. But the bellyache they could get from 'giving in' and sleeping around would last nine months, not to mention the headache of bringing up an unwanted child for years to come. I crossed my fingers and silently prayed that this would never happen to them. That was one time I thought it would have been so much easier if I had had boys instead of girls. I prayed that what I said would sink in, and wished there were a guarantee that it would. I didn't try to shove my advice down their throats and exact a promise of responsible behavior from them. I long ago found out that never works unless they themselves are convinced of its rightness. I tried instead to communicate my ideas as something they might pay serious attention to as being sensible for them, since they came from their mother, who had more experience than they had in life—a mother who loved them and was deeply concerned for their welfare.

"I recommend this approach to those clients of ours who have teenage children today. What I said about sex as a special manifestation of loving and caring is even more relevant today, and applies equally to teenage boys and girls. Considering the dangerous sexual times we live in, the least that authoritative parents can do is voice this concern to their children."

5. **The challenge to come to terms with the unfinished business in your life that exists from your family background.**

It is possible today to speak about things once considered unspeakable. Until very recently it was not possible to talk in public about such experiences as growing up in an alcoholic family, being subjected to physical or emotional abuse in childhood, or being forced into an incestuous relationship with a parent or relative. Famous people, such as Oprah Winfrey, LaToya Jackson, and Roseanne Arnold, have openly shared with the public that they were sexually abused as children by family members.

Others, like Suzanne Somers and Mariette Hartley, have written books about growing up in alcoholic families.

This is a healthy explosion of openness, for such people focus attention on the fact that you are not alone if you have had similar experiences. For example, there are at least 10 million families with children and at least one alcoholic parent. And the prevalence of incest, of sexual abuse by a family member, is so great that one in four girls and one in seven boys are sexually abused by the time they are eighteen.

These traumatic events are so overwhelming that many men and women who were victimized early in their lives when they were innocent, vulnerable children have denied this reality as adults. The pain and fear and helplessness was so frightening that they felt they had to lock away their horrifying memories and even deny to themselves that those experiences ever happened simply in order to survive. As adults they would create a fantasy world for themselves. If they were asked, "How was your childhood?" their answer often would be, "Great, my parents loved me dearly, and we had wonderful times together."

But something frequently happens, usually in the late thirties or forties, during the time-is-running-out marriage, to cause this fantasy facade to start to crumble, and people begin to get in touch with the true reality of their experiences in their family of origin. There is no question that society's publicity about the millions of men and women who are adult children of alcoholics or victims of childhood incest has powerfully reinforced the belief that there is nothing to fear in remembering these experiences and that now you can eliminate them from interfering negatively in your present life. The very fact that men and women can confront the "demons" of the past when they are in their early middle years is an indication that they no longer see themselves as the little children they once were who had to bury their terror-ridden feelings in order to survive.

If you or your spouse came from a background of family alcoholism, or incest, or emotional or physical abuse, that background can have a self-destructive impact on your marriage if you are not aware of how its influences your personality and the way you relate to others. For example, an adult child of alcoholics learned, as a child, to behave in many of the following ways in order to survive in a family that was totally out of control. This list is derived from Janet Gering Woititz's fine book on the subject, *Adult Children of Alcoholics:*

1. Adult children of alcoholics guess at what normal behavior is.

2. Adult children of alcoholics have difficulty following a project through from beginning to end.

3. Adult children of alcoholics lie when it would be just as easy to tell the truth.

4. Adult children of alcoholics judge themselves without mercy.

5. Adult children of alcoholics have difficulty having fun.

6. Adult children of alcoholics take themselves very seriously.

7. Adult children of alcoholics have difficulty with intimate relationships.

8. Adult children of alcoholics overreact to changes over which they have no control.

9. Adult children of alcoholics constantly seek approval and affirmation.

10. Adult children of alcoholics usually feel that they are different from other people.

11. Adult children of alcoholics are superresponsible or superirresponsible.

12. Adult children of alcoholics are extremely loyal, even in the face of evidence that the loyalty is undeserved.

13. Adult children of alcoholics are impulsive. They tend to lock themselves into a course of action without giving serious consideration to alternative behaviors or possible consequences. This impulsivity leads to confusion, self-loathing, and loss of control over their environment. In addition, they spend an excessive amount of energy cleaning up the mess.

Should you find traces of these qualities in your own interaction with your spouse and your children, there is no need to despair, for you no longer are that helpless child at the mercy of arbitrary parental abuse. You can take charge of your own life now and expunge these traces of the past by going to a counselor who specializes in dealing with this subject and/or joining one of the many thousands of Adult Children of Alcoholics self-help groups. They can be found through the Alcoholics Anonymous organization in your community.

If you have been the victim of childhood incest and have been unaware until recently of the ways it might have shaped some of your behavior, you now have the opportunity to identify them. Perhaps you do not like being held, or have a low sense of self-esteem, or believe you are loved only because you are sexually available, or mistrust all men including your husband, or believe marriage is a power relationship in which your partner "inevitably" has to dominate you, or feel joyless because you always see life as a half-empty rather than a half-full glass, or feel a mixture of hate-love-revulsion toward the parent who sexually abused you, or experience fear-ridden flashbacks during sex, or experience an underlying depression like a black cloud that never goes away.

These are some of the bleak legacies of sexual abuse. However, you can eliminate their hold over you now that you are a knowledgeable adult. There are many excellent counselors who specialize in helping sexually abused persons, and you should be able to find one in your community. There are numerous self-help groups for adults who were sexually abused as children. You can join one by checking with the local nonprofit family service agency or mental health association in your area. And there are two excellent books on the subject that you and your spouse can read and discuss to deepen your own relationship. They are written by Laura Davis, a national authority on childhood sexual abuse. Her books are *Courage to Heal* and *Allies in Healing* (HarperCollins).

6. **The challenge to develop the courage to prevail over the unexpected tragedies in your life.**

If there is one thing we can expect from life, it is that the unexpected will happen. The unexpected may be good news, such as a new job offer or a raise, a great price on a house, a lump in the breast that is benign instead of cancerous. Or the unexpected may be tragic. There are tragedies that are often avoidable (car accidents, AIDS, lung cancer due to smoking, heart attacks from poor diets). On the other hand, unavoidable tragedies also exist and start to proliferate in the time-is-running-out marriage: the death of one or both parents; or discovery of a genetic predisposition to manic-depression or a biological tendency to develop lupus or ovarian cancer or Alzheimer's disease. However, even the avoidable tragedies are unexpected in the sense that the possibility of their happening is too painful to acknowledge to oneself (even though we know intellectually it can or will happen), so it comes as an "unexpected" shock when it does. Author William Saroyan's comment is to the point: "Everybody has got to die," he said when he was on his deathbed, "but I always believed an exception would be made in my case. Now what?"

There are no "solutions" to the tragedies inherent in life. And we as the authors of this book would be remiss if we were to offer easy answers to unanswerable questions, like, Why is this happening to me? and Why now, of all the times in my life?

We must use reserves of courage, compassion, empathy, and love to weather these events so that the pain will diminish with time rather than continue to dominate our lives.

Perhaps the most devastating and indeed unexpected tragedy in a couple's lives is the suicide of a teenage son or daughter. It is a comment on the dark times we live in that teenage suicide has tripled in the past three decades. It is, indeed, particularly horrifying when children, whose lives are supposed to be just beginning, decide instead to end their lives. It's like a crime against nature. After all, aren't parents supposed to die long before their children?

7. **The challenge to affirm and acknowledge to each other the competencies you both possess to weather the storms in this stage of your life together.**

The hopes, dreams, fears, and confusion attendant on reaching middle age need to be honestly faced by each of you and then shared. The objective here is to reinforce the present competencies both you and your spouse possess, rather than to wallow in regrets over the loss of youth. A reexamination of your past life together is in order so the two of you can assess what you have learned from the past, not what you have "lost" by growing older. Maybe it is wisdom to let go of the old definitions of "success" you held when you were younger. Maybe it is strength to realize that nothing lasts forever. Maybe the "perfect parent" is the parent who can forgive himself or herself for not being perfect, but is instead a loving and caring, strong and

tender (and occasionally fallible) role model for the children—
the good-enough parent we outlined in the previous chapter.
Maybe each of you deserves a pat on the back for adhering to
your belief in vital family values. Sacrifice, benevolent dedication to the demands of family life, persistence in the face of adversity, the nurturing of loyalty, trust, and tolerance between
partners, may be infinitely more valuable than a larger house or
the addition of a six-foot television screen. They become sources
of strength to weather present and future uncertainties instead
of signs that you are "old-fashioned."

You need this positive reinforcement because the values you
grew up with don't seem to count: like "Plan for the future." But
is there a future when it is increasingly likely that you could be
fired at a moment's notice? Or, "Take pride in your work; your
boss will always appreciate your extra ounce of effort on the
job." But what if your boss treats you like a number instead of a
human being? It's not what you know but who you know, and
the business game is rigged to freeze you in your place. "Look
forward to your later years, when you'll be respected for the wisdom you've gained and can share with the younger generation."
But respect is given only to the young; they are the ones, after
all, who have the kind of disposable income media advertisers
love to tap. So, it would seem, the older you get, the more irrelevant you become.

In your time-is-running-out marriage you may be gripped
with the feeling that it's all a con game and the American dream
is nothing more than that—a dream. Your wife becomes the
mirror of your own fears and frustrations; your husband becomes the duplicate of your insecurities. This is the time when
there is regret and guilt about the past and fear about the future,
while the present seems to be little more than a bridge between
the two. A reexamination of the quality of your life, the values
you believe in, the goals you strive for, the allegiances that bind

you to family, friends, and society is in order. In doing it you can renew each other's courage and begin the process of cutting asunder your difficulties.

## 8. The challenge to live in the present rather than in the past or the future.

If much of your time is now spent regretting what might have been, you are living in the past. If you are always worried and fearful of what could happen tomorrow or the day after, you are living in the future. But what you do today will soon become part of your past and will also determine your future. The English novelist Charles Morgan points out, "To live in the present does not imply rashness or irresponsibility or selfishness; it is not an act of hedonism or of cowardly escape. It is to live with instant appreciation of the good in life and in freedom from obsessive anxiety."

Living in the here and now means ending your procrastination about acting on goals that you feel are of vital importance to fulfilling your life. Have you always wanted to play an instrument, learn a new sport, take a course, visit a foreign country, change your job? Now is the time for deeds instead of words.

Whenever our clients experience regret over the past or fear of what the future will bring, a poet can wake them up to living in the present. Here is the wake-up poem by Christopher Logue we share with those clients:

### Good Taste

Travelling, a man met a tiger, so . . .
he ran. And the tiger ran after him
thinking: How fast I am . . .
But the road thought: How long I am . . .
then they came to a cliff, and the man
grabbed at an ash-root and swung down

over its edge. Above his knuckles, the tiger;
at the foot of the cliff, its mate. Two mice,
one black, one white, began to gnaw the root.
And by the traveller's head grew one
juicy strawberry. So . . . hugging the root
the man reached out and plucked the fruit:
How sweet it tasted!

*Chapter Seven*

# The Is-This-All-There-Is? Marriage

❦

As fast as fifty snaps of your fingers, fifty years go by. If it seemed that you were "suddenly" forty, fifty has arrived with lightning speed. Not only does it seem that you have been mugged by time, you don't even know what fifty "means."

We have identified this fifth marriage of your marriage as the Is-this-all-there-is? marriage because the period we are dealing with, between fifty and sixty-five, is viewed by our society as a nowhere state: too old to be considered young, too young to be considered old. A vivid example of how this confusion about what fifty-plus means to one's sense of self was spelled out in an article written by K. O. Eckland when he had just turned fifty-five:

A short time ago, I went hurtling through the 55 barrier without a fanfare or a crash of timpani, not even a token sonic boom. It was a date that this aging Aquarian had anticipated with no small amount of trepidation, likening it to the 21st birthday when I left the category of "teenager" to officially become a man. Now I was about to become a "senior citizen" though some years still remote from Social Security benefits. After 35 years of being non-descript, after successfully making the transition from freckles to liver spots, I once more had a category to cling to.

It should have been a somewhat special occasion, but it was merely another day to be crossed off the calendar. . . . There was no significant aftershock that morning. I looked at the face in the bathroom mirror, and it didn't appear to be all that much different. . . .

I didn't suddenly feel 55, maybe I never will. For one thing, I don't know the ground rules. I don't know how I'm supposed to feel or act. Do I go out and buy my first rocking chair or a supply of Grecian Formula? Or a hot-water bottle? Do I dig up a copy of Hoyle's *Pocket Guide to Bingo?* Should I set my affairs in order (a 10-year project right there)? How do I mold myself into a cartoon character of the senior citizen that the outside world expects? Or should I follow the example of my cadre of over-the-hill friends and act as if nothing ever happened?

Hopefully, I can spend my remaining years catching up on the trappings of a new environment. For openers, I plan on stridently contesting the "citizen" label that I'm about to be saddled with: I hate to see 55 years of patri-otic loyalty to the United States of America needing such blatant jurisdiction. Luckily, I'm not a greencarder, or I could be a "senior alien." Bad enough as it is.

Then I'll try to find the supreme authority that can tell me where seniordom actually begins. Not everyone sub-scribes to 55. Even our government is vague about the whole thing. Social Security refers to 62 out of one side of its mouth, 65 out of the other. And our elder statesmen are toying with the idea of moving the retirement age up a few years. More liberal minds accept a threshold as low as 50 but I have yet to find any authoritative guide that names the square that I'm standing on. . . .

One thing for certain, I'd hate to be 21 now and faced with what our junior citizens are up against. I like being right where I am, double nickels and all.

Considering the alternatives, I'd better.

K. O. Eckland is a former art director of the *Los Angeles Times* who was the editor of *California Senior* magazine when this article appeared in the *Times* (22 February 1983).

He did not retire "from" something, he retired "to" something new that injected new excitement into his life, rather than old regrets.

We have both experienced the feelings Mr. Eckland so eloquently describes. And we have discovered to our own personal delight—a delight the 30 million other people in the fifty-to-sixty-five age bracket can also discover—that the fifty-plus generation is in many ways more alive, flexible, resilient, innovative, risk-taking, imaginative, and achievement-oriented than any other age group. Instead of this period being an "Is that all there is?" way station on the downhill road to the grave, it is an exciting time for self-renewal and marriage renewal.

We have certainly experienced this reality in our own lives: Mel was in his fifties when he wrote his very first book, which became an international best-seller; Pat became a seminar leader, lecturer, and writer in psychology in that time also. Neither of us had ever done that kind of work before, so we know from personal experience that the fifties can indeed be a liberating instead of demeaning time in life.

However, in order to re-create yourself in your fifties you will have to reject society's absurd stereotype of you as part of a nowhere generation. That stereotype can be the virus that will cause new triangles in your marriage.

# *The Typical Marriage Triangles of the Is-This-All-There-Is? Marriage*

## *The Boomerang Triangle*

Free at last! Your children are grown up and on their own. An end to the economic burden of raising kids means now you can enjoy yourselves without feeling any further need for sacrifice. Hurrah for the "empty nest"! (The pain parents in their fifties are "supposed" to feel when children leave home has been highly exaggerated.)

Unfortunately, that freedom is frequently more fantasy than reality, given today's economic insecurity and the rate of breakup of young people's marriages. Because jobs are in short supply, a son or daughter may live with you long after he or she graduates from high school or college (to save money, or because he or she is unable to find a job and can't afford a place of his or her own). Or your daughter (and grandchild) may arrive on your doorstep after a divorce has left her penniless.

These adult children have been called "boomerang kids," because they have returned home after trying to make it on their own. Most of them would much prefer living on their own; they don't want to burden their parents, but find they have no other choice. If they and their parents recognize the situation as temporary, it shouldn't disrupt the parents' marriage. If it lasts too long, and nothing is said about rules and limits and what the parents expect of these boomerang children, a boomerang triangle of frustration, resentment, and fear will be created, in which the parents' number one focus will be the children who never leave home rather than each other.

## The Menopause Triangle

Though menopause can occur as early as the late thirties, the typical time is the early fifties. Just as the onset of menstruation was the most significant change in a girl's life, so too the advent of menopause profoundly affects a woman's physical and psychological sense of self.

Because menopause means an end to your periods, are you no longer a "complete," woman because you are no longer able to ovulate? Even in today's more enlightened times, that distorted view of menopause is the attitude too many women inflict upon themselves—to the detriment of their own self-images and their marriages.

Similarly, men in their fifties may hear that there is such a thing as a "male" menopause and believe they are also victims of this event. They are liable to exaggerate the fact that, because they are somewhat less able to achieve and sustain an erection and ejaculate less frequently, they are no longer "complete" men. This relatively minor result of the aging process can have a devastatingly negative effect on a man's self-image if he believes he has lost his attractiveness and competency because of it. If indeed he feels his wife can no longer regard him as the number one person in her life (just as she may feel about herself because of menopause), the relationship between them can deteriorate.

If they consider these normal processes of aging as "diseases" signifying that the end of life is near, they will create the menopause triangle, and life together will become a joyless enterprise of mutual discontent.

## The Self-pity Triangle

In the self-pity triangle, both of you feel you are living in loneliness together, that you are just habits to each other. It's comforting to believe that your present situation is all due to "the breaks"—the rotten state of the world, the way your parents screwed up your life, the selfishness of your spouse and children. You feel it's all the fault of forces beyond your control, so you're exempt from any personal responsibility for the condition you are in. And if you have a physical illness, you may ascribe it entirely to the pressures of your job, rather than recognizing that you never attempted to control your weight or change your diet or do anything to mitigate the effect those pressures had on your body. But this kind of self-comfort, consisting entirely of sadness and a sense of futility, is a poor substitute for the love you really need and want.

## The Rose-colored-Past Triangle

If your present life feels barren, you can always retreat into the past; in the rose-colored-past triangle, the past becomes a substitute for your spouse. You convince yourself that life was good then and that that was the best of times compared with now.

As you spend more and more time reliving past glories, the longer your list of everything-was-better-then grows. There is a significant element of truth in these remembrances, and pride in the past is justified. However, you create a falsified picture of the past when you erase from your mind all the difficulties, pressures, and tensions that coexisted with the pleasures. Your vision of the past then becomes an excuse and a justification for the helplessness and disenchantment you feel about your present life. You overlook the very important lesson you could learn from reviewing your past: the lesson that you survived into the present because you were competent and still are, even though you may ignore that fact today.

This escape into the past is usually reinforced with increasing amounts of alcohol, tranquilizers, or other drugs of choice. The present seems easier to take and the past grows rosier and rosier as the drugs work their effect. There are over 15 million problem drinkers in this country, with a heavy concentration in the fifty-to-sixty-five age group, and Americans consume 5 billion pills each year for relief of everyday tensions. These "solutions," of course, can become serious problems that will intensify marital unhappiness rather than remedy it.

## The Hypochondria Triangle

If you feel rejected because your spouse no longer regards you as the most important person in his or her life, it is tempting to give your imagined illnesses number one status in your own life: your retaliation for feeling rejected takes the form of a love affair with your illness. The tender loving care you give to every minute, harmless change in your body's daily functions provides interest, excitement, and drama in a life otherwise bereft of those qualities. Danger lurks everywhere—in your breathing; your heartbeat; your skin, bones, stomach, and brain. Those new sunburn freckles really be skin cancer; that back pain that happened only once may mean your spinal cord is damaged; that headache today may be the first stage of a stroke; that heartburn after a heavy meal may be a minor heart attack.

In Sherlock Holmes fashion, you identify the disease and drag it off to the doctor's office for judgment. It matters not that the doctor dismisses your fears. You've proved to yourself that you caught your enemy in time. And tomorrow another symptom may arise, so you must be continually alert, on guard. The doctor's bills may mount because of unnecessary visits, but those bills can become a source of pride, because they validate your acute detection skills.

Your hypochondria at least gets you attention from others. How can it be otherwise when you voice your panic and announce in loving detail the symptoms and progression of the many diseases you've read about? You're up-to-date because the first page you turn to in your weekly newsmagazine is the page on new medical developments. Eventually, however, you may find yourself more isolated from people than ever before, because there will come a time when you say "the sky is falling" once too often. Prudent attention to your health and regular doctor's visits when appropriate are sensible. But hypochondria is of a different order. For the panic over your health is simply the cover story you will use to hide from yourself the panic you feel about the quality of the life you are living.

### The One-Last-Chance-in-Life Triangle

In another triangle, the third party is your obsession with time. You feel that time is running out at an astounding rate (far more so than in your fourth marriage). "Will there be any life in the time you have left?" you hear your mind asking endlessly. If the children have left home and have not returned and your aged parents are not living with you, you and your spouse may find the empty nest unbearable because now that you have to pay attention to each other you find that nothing is left in the relationship but the sheer habit of living together. And then there's the panic you may feel that death is just around the corner. And you imagine it's almost certain that as you move toward your sixties you will become disabled and lose everything. This combination can produce the fantasy that it is time for your one last chance for happiness—by running away from it all.

Instead of affairs, husbands and wives these days may decide to leave their marriages permanently and seek out someone else to live with or marry. Or they may decide it would be great to live alone or move to a place they've always wanted to live or establish a new career in a different field. If, indeed, the marriage is, by now, nothing but a piece of paper, then the decision to break up might prove beneficial to both parties. But if this decision is based on panic reactions to the normal changes that growing older generates, your "one last chance for happiness" may simply turn out to be another disillusioning experience. You may have thought you were escaping your problems but find that you yourself are the real problem. All that may change is the scenery; what you gain may be nothing more than a new environment for your old fears to flourish in.

### The Grandchild Triangle

In the grandchild triangle, the number one person in your life becomes your grandchild or grandchildren. If boredom predominates, or the feeling that "there's nothing much left in our relationship," the advent of a grandchild may seem like an opportunity to fill the void inside with love and affection. Nurturing and caring for the infant will make you feel needed and wanted. Here at least is a person beholden to you. The tendency in this triangle is for grandmothers or grandfathers to become busybodies and pests in their grown children's eyes.

When a grandchild is used as a substitute for the love and excitement a couple should find with each other, this triangle can only cause eventual estrangement from one's own children and grandchildren. Your grown children may wish to exploit your baby-sitting services, but they will feel angry and distressed should you become overconcerned and overinvolved with their children, for they will consider the parenting function as their own prideful responsibility. Solicited suggestions may be welcome, but backseat driving is not. And your spouse, viewing the grandchildren as competitors for your attention, may feel jealous, cold, and distant toward them and you as a consequence. Instead of filling the void in your life, the grandchild triangle will enlarge the void.

### The Pet Triangle

If you feel your favorite household pet provides you with the love, affection, and attention you are not receiving from your spouse, you are in the pet triangle. You may spend endless time patiently feeding and grooming and playing with your special dog or cat. The names you use may sound like a lover's names: *Darling, Honey, Sweets, Cutey.* The affection you demonstrate can look like a courtship as you hug, kiss, stroke, fondle, and cuddle your pet. And there are now three of you in bed—you, your spouse, and your pet. You may worry over the shape and size and decoration of your pet's living quarters as much as if you were remodeling your own house or apartment.

Your efforts are returned in kind; there is your adoring pet, attentive to your slightest movement, sad when you leave, over-joyed when you return home. Here, at least, is someone you can always count on, somebody who always regards you as number one. The jealousy and anger this can activate in an ignored hus-band or wife is proportionate to the amount of attention show-ered on a pet. Grumblings of "If my wife had her way, I'd be eating dog food and her dog would be eating steak" are not unusual. And stories of an irate wife or husband drowning the spouse's cat or shooting the spouse's dog are not uncommon. To love animals for what they are makes sense. But to love them for what they are not (they may be many things, but they are not human beings) will never fill the void inside you that aches for adult human caring and affection.

## The Television Triangle

That Cyclops in your living room is the third party in the television triangle. Here is something that is as faithful as a pet, always on call to meet your needs, and requiring no effort on your part. Just push a button, and someone is there to make you laugh, to make you feel tender and loving, to become your friend, to take you around the world, to thrill and excite you—everything your spouse doesn't do. The two of you may sit together staring at the screen for half a dozen hours a night and yet be in separate worlds, nursing different fantasies. Some cou-ples scatter TV sets around the house as if they were peanuts—one for the kitchen, another for the bedroom, den, workshop. Quarrels over what programs to watch can then be resolved by walking into another room. If there is only one set, bored couples can add some excitement to their lives by fighting over which programs to watch. But it's all so unsatisfying. TV isn't used selectively for a bit of passive recreation; it's used instead as an answer to a question it can't possibly answer. That question is, Where can I find that person who once saw me as number one in his or her life?

## The Retirement-Dream Triangle

As you move closer to your sixties, the retirement issue can turn into a triangle. You may become enamored of your own dream of what retirement should be like and ignore the needs of your spouse, who may have a different dream. You may want to sell the house and move to a modest condominium; your spouse may wish to hold onto the house because of its memories. You may envisage buying a boat and taking a trip around the world; your spouse may be prone to seasickness or want to take courses at the local college instead.

You may say, with fingers crossed, that you want to retire early, because you know that your spouse doesn't want to wait until you're sixty-five. However, you fear for your economic future in these tumultuous times. And besides, what in the world will you do once you no longer have the routine of going to work each morning? Both of you may fear retirement and wish to postpone it indefinitely because you associate retirement with very old age and death. Perhaps your father withered away and died a year after he took his pension—and you fear that may happen to you. Or your mother might have mourned over her loss of function as a mother and a housewife and died from lack of stimulation—and you fear that may happen to you. Most of these thoughts, hopes, and fears may remain unspoken between you until the inevitable time comes when they can no longer be nurtured in silence. Unless they are constructively dealt with, your conflicting retirement dreams and nightmares may further estrange you from each other.

## Your Mutual Development Challenges

You will have lived at least two-thirds of your life by the time you enter your is-this-all-there-is? marriage. In all that time, you have accumulated a treasury of experience, much of which you may never have examined or evaluated realistically. This is true of all couples to a greater or lesser extent. We tend to live in our marriages with tunnel vision. Just coping with and surviving each day's problems requires so much energy and attention that we fail to see the forest for the trees. We get into the habit of believing that one day, in essence, is like any other day, that our marriage is just the same old series of rituals and routines that will repeat themselves from now until eternity. But now it's twenty-five or thirty years after your wedding, and time slaps you in the face (as it does all of us) and says, "Stop sleepwalking, wake up! Can't you see that you've both undergone enormous changes in your lives in all those years? You once thought and acted as if you would live forever. Now you know that is not true, so why don't you use the time you have left in the best possible ways?"

Your mutual development challenges at this time in your life are directed toward answering these questions that time poses. The major challenges are the following:

**1. The challenge to mine the gold residing in your past experiences.**

Contrary to what you may think, your past is not a fixed image engraved in stone. In the words of the psychologist Herman Feifel, "The past is an image that changes with ourselves. . . .

In human beings present behavior is dependent not only on the past, but more potently, perhaps, on orientation toward future events. Indeed, what a person seeks to become may well, at times, decide to what he attends in his past." This means that if you view the present as a time of despair, helplessness, and hopelessness that will never end, you may, in order to comfort yourself, remember your past as all great and happy and wonderful. Because you have the sense that the future is bleak and scary, the past becomes the equivalent of a drug high. Nostalgia then becomes a substitute for coping effectively with your present problems.

If, however, you see the present time in your life as a time in which you can, to a significant extent, shape your life for the better and improve your relationship with your spouse, you will view your past in an entirely different light. You will focus on how much you've learned over the years about yourself and others and about the ways of the world. You will concentrate on how you triumphed over past adversities, and that will give you the courage and confidence to triumph over present ones. You will compare who you were in the past with who you are today in order to determine the ways in which you are now better, more skillful, and effective—and will derive courage from what you see. Instead of obsessively worrying over present losses in your life, you will focus on the gains you have made and will continue to make. You will see that your past was also a time of losses and that adversity not only did not kill you, it made you stronger.

If your physical condition has worsened, know that such changes may be reversible. If you are not as fleet and muscular as you once were, you are by contrast more skillful and effective in the ways you use your energy. If you are not as intense and spontaneous as you once were, you are now more thoughtful and wiser and less prone to impulsive decision making. In this view, an inventory of the internal resources you had in the past becomes a spur to the betterment of your life in the present. The challenge for you and your spouse is to opt for present and future possibilities for yourselves rather than becoming grave tenders to your past.

When we find couples we work with wallowing in regrets, we hand them a copy of this little story about two monks; we believe there is great value in practicing its meaning:

### Muddy Road

Tanzan and Ekido were once traveling together
down a muddy road. A heavy rain was still
falling.
Coming around a bend, they met a lovely girl
in a silk kimono and sash, unable to cross
the intersection.
"Come on, girl," said Tanzan at once.
Lifting her in his arms, he carried her over
the mud.
Ekido did not speak again until that night
when they reached a lodging temple. Then he
no longer could restrain himself. "We monks
don't go near females," he told Tanzan,
"especially not young and lovely ones. It is
dangerous. Why did you do that?"
"I left the girl there," said Tanzan. "You
are still carrying her."

2. **The challenge to improve your relationships with your children now that they are markedly different from what they once were.**

Your children are now adults, but difficulties will arise if you continue to see and treat them as little children. Many couples feel the need to transform their twenty-five or thirty-year-old sons or daughters into the ten-year-olds they once were. This need springs partly out of habit; they were children for eighteen years, so it's all too easy to slip into telling them what to do, explaining the obvious, and monitoring their intimate lives as if they were not grown-ups today. But this need can also spring from a desire to turn back the clock, to act as if you are still the young, powerful parent whose word is law. If you've been suffering the feeling that no one thinks you're the greatest person in the world anymore, you can at least assert your authority over your children so that they will.

But it doesn't work that way. Your adult children will only resent your authoritarian attitude and then feel guilty for holding such negative feelings toward you. Treat your children as the adults they are. They want to be your friends as well as your blood relations. They want their ideas, their hopes and fears, to be treated with the respect and consideration you would give to any other thoughtful adult. The parental tie will never disappear, but it can now be meshed with a friendship based on the equality of adults relating to adults.

This is the time in your lives to recognize and appreciate the valuable life lessons your children have taught the both of you:

- They taught you what responsibility means, that you could accept the duties and obligations of being parents and could be depended upon to fulfill them.

- They taught you how to listen, not only to their voices, but to their feelings and behavior as well.

- They taught you endurance, patience, and sacrifice—the survival qualities needed to prevail over life's difficulties.

- They taught you to discover the reserves of unexpected strength within you to cope with their illnesses and their antisocial behavior.

- They taught you empathy, for in trying to understand them you had to put yourself in their place.

- They taught you joy and delight as you saw them successfully respond to your positive suggestions about how to solve their problems.

- They taught you that the aliveness and curiosity they exhibited as children are two of the most valuable things in life—that these qualities can enable you to be psychologically young forever.

These are the gifts for living your children have given you. In your fifties you can appreciate, perhaps for the first time, how enormously they have enriched your lives not only as parents but as whole human beings.

### 3. The challenge to deepen your relationship with your parents.

The fact that your parents may now be fragile requires you to be the strong one in your family. They need to be treated with the care and consideration they once gave you. This does not mean sacrificing your own life for them, but it may mean some temporary sacrifice of time, effort, and involvement with them to assure them of maximum care and love in their old age. Recognize that, in all likelihood, they wish to avoid placing the burden of their welfare on you and want to continue to have an independent existence themselves. They fear most of all the possibility that their physical deterioration may make them rely on you more than they wish to.

You cannot give them the assurance they need if you feel hostile or resentful toward them or if you feel guilty because you don't devote all your time and attention to them. In either case, your own emotional disarray will have a negative effect on your parents (who will feel unwanted and unloved) and on your spouse (who will feel as if your parents have displaced him or her in your feelings). A role reversal has taken place: it seems as if you are the parent and your parents the children. The challenge here is to become aware of these feelings inside you and not let them dominate the way you live. After all, your parents are not children (they are more sensitive and alert and intelligent than you give them credit for), and you are not their parents but a concerned adult whose affection for his or her parents sensitizes you to their needs and at the same time enables you to establish limits so that their needs do not overwhelm your relationship with your spouse.

The challenge to improve your relationship with your parents is a challenge to know them in greater depth. This is the time to learn more about your family's roots, to learn more about what your parents were really like when you were growing up, rather than what you thought about them at the time. You may be surprised, delighted, and warmed by the revelations you can elicit from long conversations with your parents. After all, when you were growing up, these people were not only your parents; they were also adults managing marriage, work, and the rest of life.

### 4. The challenge for women in their fifties to get in touch with their own personal power.

Because our society still continues to value the physical beauty of youth as the most important measures of a woman's value and worth, the beauty of women middle-aged and older is either denied, ignored, or demeaned. We will continue to live with a double standard as long as the media send out signals that men in their fifties can still be considered "attractive" and "mature," while women of the same age are "over the hill" or "past their prime." Unfortunately, too many women in their fifties continue to victimize themselves by believing in this stereotype.

If you don't feel good about yourselves, how can you feel good about your marriage? Marital happiness today is based on gender equality, on two equal people feeling good about themselves and each other and sharing a constructive life. If you believe that because you are now in your fifties you are flawed, imperfect, "less-than," the marriage will suffer.

Pat has led many educational women's groups on this subject (for women of fifty to sixty-five). Here is what she has to say:

The fifties are a time of dramatic change, a restless time for women now that menopause has arrived. It's a time when women feel different. As a woman you're changing. You have learned much, stored much information during the years, so on the one hand you feel like a powerhouse, but on the other hand, you see society pushing you into a backseat. People in their twenties and thirties aren't polite to you. You're the last to be waited on in restaurants and first to be cut off on the highway.

Because of the way you're treated, you're liable to see this as confirmation that you "deserve" to be treated in this demeaning way. You go shopping in department stores and get into a dressing room, only to find that what used to look good on you doesn't anymore. Your body has changed. "What's all this flab on my arms and hips and thighs?" you ask yourself. You start to think you need a complete overhaul (My God, I need to get active to get this flab off!).

The food you used to buy and eat doesn't taste as good as it once did. Why did peanut butter once taste so satisfying but now sticks in your throat like a used tire, refusing to be digested? The nuts you used to love now sound like grinding machinery in your stomach.

You look in the mirror and think, "Why are there lines over my lips, and the new ones around my eyes and neck? My hands—what are all those new brown spots on the backs of them? My bra size has tripled, yet it's all flab, not muscular the way my breasts once were. Help!"

If you whip yourself into disliking what you see, you do have the choice of changing yourself instead of feeling like a helpless victim. That's the way you demonstrate to yourself, your husband, and the world that the fifties can be the best time in your life, rather than the worst. Here is what I recommend to women in their fifties to get in touch with the powerful person inside them:

*a.* Eliminate the notion that you lose your attractiveness and femininity once you pass menopause. We can be sexy—and enjoy sex!—until the day we die. Mel and I always recommend to women and men in their fifties to get the most accurate and up-to-date information on sex and aging that they possibly can. We suggest they both read and discuss the chapter on sex and aging in the Kinsey Institute's *New Report on Sex,* so that they can understand the physiological changes they are undergoing. Otherwise, there is a tendency for both wives and husbands to frighten themselves to death by falsely believing their lives are now at a dead end.

*b.* Find exercise that you love to do, such as walking, swimming, golfing, bowling, tennis. Make sure you consistently work at the program at least three times a week.

*c.* Concentrate on proper nutrition. Food today can be tasty as well as healthful—low-fat cheese, graham crackers, gelatin, light ice cream substitutes, lots of fish, poultry, fruit, and vegetables. Read labels, and avoid nonnutritional products with palm oil and cottonseed oil.

*d.* Rediscover college. You will find many, many students your age at your local school. Learn new things, meet new people, make new friends.

*e.* Smell the flowers. Go to places you can afford, like fairs, picnics, get-togethers with friends.

*f.* Get involved in a political organization so that you can change the things in society you feel need changing, instead of waiting for others to change them (because they never will).

*g.* See what needs improvement in your neighborhood or city, and join an organization that is trying to make that improvement happen.

*h.* Volunteer at schools or with a Big Sister group to help this generation of children become fired with a desire to be responsible, creative, and excited about life.

*i.* Read good books, become informed politically, make your representatives in Congress understand that women such as you will no longer tolerate being treated like second-class citizens.

*j.* Think of fifty as the beginning of middle age, rather than old age, because today that's the reality of the adult age revolution. In the words of Jean Monnet, a French writer, "It is only when we climb that we see new horizons."

5. **The challenge to widen the range of your experiences in life rather than contract them.**

Our research has confirmed that the fifty-plus generation is in many ways more alive, flexible, resilient, innovative, risk-taking, imaginative, and achievement-oriented than any other age group. Instead of treating this period of life as a way station on a downhill road to the grave, you can make it a highway to new achievements. We have already shared this idea with the general public in a series of fifteen half-hour programs we created for TV, called "Join the Group," which was shown nationally over the Cable Health Network. This series dealt specifically with the challenges facing people who are between fifty and sixty-five and how they can be met successfully. Here is what they had to say for themselves:

### Beyond the Menopause: A Time for Self-Renewal

Sharon, who is fifty-three, says, "I had quite a hard time with my menopause. I can remember being so emotional. I cried at the teensiest problem. My teenagers were mad because I was so possessive and 'mothering.' And I was. I'd get into the car and follow them. I'd call and make sure they went where they said they were going. And I tell you, these were kids seventeen and eighteen years old. Finally my daughter talked me into going to see a doctor. Well, I did go to see the doctor, who confirmed that I was going through menopause. He didn't tell me anything else. He didn't tell me why I felt so creepy. He just told me that he was going to put me on hormones and that they just put women on hormones to pamper us because we get so emotional over everything. It was so patronizing. I could have hit him! Now I look back at everything. I've apologized to my children and husband for being so overwrought all those years. Now, if anything, it's been a very sexually freeing experience. I've never felt so complete as a woman. I feel that finally I can let go and enjoy sex. My husband loves the change, and it's really been responsible for putting the life back into our marriage."

There is no male equivalent physiologically to what women experience during menopause. The physical changes in men in this age bracket are modest but often highly exaggerated by those men who believe that their lives are over. These are the men who have experienced a hardening of their psychological arteries, not their physical ones.

Marvin, age fifty-four, tells how he overcame that self-imposed psychological hurdle: "Around fifty, I definitely went through a change. It wasn't physical, but it had a lot to do with my sense of self-worth. I felt that I was no longer the virile man I was at twenty and thirty. I really became aware of that. I left my wife and started really stretching my sexual 'legs.' I went through two years of this, until one night while I was having my dinner, which consisted of peanut butter, cheese crackers, and coffee (I was too lazy to go out and get something and cook it, and I was tired of restaurants), I realized how lonely I was. None of the women I was seeing really turned me on mentally. It was all so empty. So I called my wife and started to court her again, and six months later she took me back.

"I look at sex differently now. It's no longer a numbers game with me. I wanted to return to my wife because it finally dawned on me that there was nothing to prove. Love, trust, sharing the joys and sorrows of life together were the most important things. Screwing around made me feel empty instead. So if I sometimes fail to ejaculate or have an erection, I now see it as no big deal. I no longer think my wife won't love me for that. Now maybe we have sex three or four times a month, and that's fine. When we have it, we enjoy it more than we used to. I'm no longer under pressure to perform. I have to laugh, because I put myself under that pressure! It's been a very freeing thing for me to eliminate that hangup I had."

In one's fifties the meaning of love and the quality of one's marriage can be defined far beyond the measure of sexual gratification. Here is what Malcolm, who is fifty-eight, has to say on this subject: "What I find most important in my relationship with my wife is a feeling of closeness and caring. That's what I define as 'love.' I've heard one hundred definitions of love, but that's the best one. I've been married thirty years, and my love for my wife is stronger now than it was twenty years ago. My needs were different then, not stronger or weaker.

"I used to need and want sex. Women were receptacles for men. It's different now. We've been through so much together—when I had my heart attack five years ago and she was there every minute caring for me; raising the kids; saving for our vacations; helping each other's sick parents; surviving when I was unemployed and her not putting me down once because I wasn't a good provider then. It's caring for each other, remembering how we struggled to make a good life with each other. It's sharing our lives, which is far more important than 'getting it on.' It's what I call love."

### Health Renewal: Making Friends with Your Own Body

When you turn fifty your birthday presents don't have to be obesity, hypertension, emphysema, heart attack, strokes, and physical debilitation. You can minimize such possibilities.

Loretta, a fifty-three-year-old legal secretary, tells of her own self-renewal: "I'm only five feet three inches tall and very small-boned, and I had been used to eating whatever and whenever I wished. But I started to gain weight as I turned fifty. And before I knew it, I weighed over two hundred pounds. I found the more I weighed, the more I had to eat to keep me going. Sitting down and eating a five-pound bag of candy or a two-pound box of cookies was nothing to me. I looked twenty years older than I actually was and felt terrible. I couldn't walk very far without feeling faint. I became diabetic. My heart pounded. My ankles swelled. I was a mess. People used to think I was my husband's mother. Doctors told me to lose weight, but none of the diets I tried did me any good. Oh, I'd lose maybe twenty pounds, but then something would set me off emotionally, and I would start eating again.

"I have three beautiful children, and my daughter used to model. She was a centerfold. The photographer was over at the house showing us the proof sheets, and one of my sons came in with a friend. The friend started to look at the pictures and was obviously quite impressed. He asked who the girl was, and I told him she was my daughter. 'That's your daughter!?' he said, in a tone that told me he couldn't believe that such a lovely girl could come out of a bloated wreck like me.

"I decided that I had to change. I started to go to a weight doctor who put me on a rigid diet, but one that would allow me to lose weight without becoming too weak. He put me on diet pills, which helped me through the first week, but then I found that I could maintain the diet without them. In five months, I was down to one hundred forty pounds. I remember going to see my daughter, who was on a promotional tour, and from a distance she didn't recognize me for a moment. I finally got down to one hundred twelve pounds, which is about right for my height and build, but my skin hung on me grotesquely. My face, in particular, looked terrible. I decided to get a face-lift. It made me look twenty years younger.

"To get my body back in some sort of shape, I started going to a gym and attending jazz dancing classes. I also went out and got a job. Today I feel younger than I did twenty years ago, and I certainly look better. The diabetes went away with the weight, and the tendency I had toward being high-strung went away, too. Now that I have my self-esteem back, I feel much more confident that whatever I want to do, I can do. I'm now taking jazz piano lessons and am thinking about a second career as a jazz pianist or accompanist."

Mark, who is fifty-six, also took personal responsibility for transforming himself: "When I turned fifty, I had hypertension and high blood pressure. I was on medicine that had an adverse affect on my overall health. I was a workaholic and thirty pounds overweight, working sixteen hours a day, drinking and smoking, and on a course to a heart attack at fifty-four if I made it to that (my father died at that age). Four months and twenty-three days after my fiftieth birthday, I made a New Year's resolution to lose the weight. I played three sets of tennis the next morning and had to go to bed for the rest of the day. Two months later, I climbed on the scale and weighed two pounds more than I had on New Year's. I felt if I didn't do something now, there was no point in living. So I told my wife, 'Get me to a fat farm.'

"I went to a fitness resort, where they gave me a diet and exercise plan. Cold turkey I stopped drinking and smoking. By the time I left, I had thrown away my blood pressure medicine and gone from 30 percent to 15 percent body fat. Thirty pounds lighter. I was on a natural high, better than liquor and cigarettes.

"I said then that I want to feel like this forever, and I do feel that way now, five years later. Because I've kept to the same health habits I learned there. I work at it. I learned in my business that there is no such thing as a free lunch, so why should it be any different when it comes to taking care of my health? Sure, I work at it. I've also stopped working sixteen hours a day. I'm spending more time with my wife, doing things we like—playing tennis, gardening, seeing a good show. When I say I feel younger today than I did at fifty—or forty, for that matter—I'm not kidding myself. I've more energy and am in far better shape than I was then. Isn't that the test of feeling young?"

### Alcohol and Drugs: Turning on to Life Instead of Illusion

When life seems hopeless, there is always the temptation to create an alternative existence by drowning oneself in alcohol or drugs, whether you are a teenager, a young adult, middle-aged, or older. Alcohol and drugs are ageless escapes.

Dan, an actor just turned fifty, tells of this turnaround from alcohol to life: "I used to drink, smoke grass, and take uppers, but it was mostly booze. I felt I needed something to cope with life. I drank in the morning; I drank constantly, even when I worked. I didn't realize it, but I was getting a poor reputation, and then it started to affect my work and my ability to get jobs. Of course, at first, I didn't believe it was all happening. I was angry with them and blamed the casting directors and producers. I accused them of having a grudge against me. I was the innocent victim, and that made me drink all the more. I truly didn't think I had a problem. But then I did a play, and I had a blackout right in the middle of the performance. If you had asked me what my name was, I could not have told you. Right then, I realized that it was affecting my work and that there was some substance to the rumors about me. I joined an alcohol support group, and they helped me break the habit.

"I think the whole experience made me more attuned to life and what's really going on. I realized that I will always be an alcoholic because I have the disease. But it's not going to affect my life again."

### Death and Dying: Facts of Life

Death can happen at any age, but it becomes more and more a real fact of life as one lives through one's fifties and early sixties, when many more friends, relatives, and loved ones will die. Confrontation with such deaths can become an affirmation of life and an incentive to make the most of the time you have left on earth without panic and fear.

This happened to Elaine, who is fifty-nine: "When my father was dying, they had him tied to the bed. He really wanted to die. They had to feed him intravenously. He was a doctor, and he knew what was happening. I had to stay with him all night to make sure he didn't pull the needles out of his arm. He had had eight strokes. I blamed God, but then I realized that you must be able to let go of someone if you really love them. You must accept them as they are, and when they die, you must realize that it is meant to be.

"I am currently grieving the dying of a close friend. She is completing a very long and satisfying life. She is truly suffering. I think death is a suffering to be borne. I was thinking that the other night as I sat with her, and suddenly I felt very much at one with her. I now feel a lot better about my own mortality. It's the natural way of things. I'm not going to speed things up, but I certainly plan to take things a little easier. I would like to get to know my husband and my son better and maybe do some traveling. It was a very positive experience, as it's helped me come to terms with the reality of death."

Hal, who is sixty-one, is now taking care of his father, who is eighty-four and dying of lung cancer: "I want to tell you, it's tough to watch your father waste away and die. I've got a sister and a brother, but they both live out of state, so that leaves me pretty much the one who is there with him every day.

"It's a helluva responsibility, and I just thank God I'm capable of being there for him, to give him whatever solace I can. Yes, there are times when I wonder why I had to be the one to do this—What exactly is the lesson I'm supposed to be getting from this? Perhaps God is trying to 'alert' me. Because as much studying and reading as I've done, I guess nothing is quite as 'alerting' as watching somebody face death, particularly my father whom I love. By 'alerting' I mean God is telling me to remember that nothing lasts forever, including me, which is something I never really believed before. Also to treasure my wife and sons and friends more. I'm the kind of person who's always found it difficult to express my feelings. Of course, I love my wife and kids, but I never tell them that—or tell my friends how much I value them. But I'm telling them now."

These men and women are living confirmation of Dr. Robert Lifton's evaluation of this time in life:

> There is a special quality of life-power available only to those seasoned by struggles of four or more decades. That seasoning includes extensive cultivation of images and forms having to do with love and caring, with experienced parenthood, with teaching and mentorship, with work combinations and professional creativity, with responses to intellectual and artistic images around one, and above all with humor and a sense of the absurd. . . . the life-power of this stage can be especially profound.

## 6. The challenge to prepare realistically for the critical years ahead.

This is the time in life when the unthinkable needs to be thought about—the unthinkable possibility that either you or your spouse might die in the not-too-distant future, the unthinkable possibility that retirement might soon become a reality rather than just a vague light-years-away dream. Because women, on the average, outlive men by eight years, a wife may very well be jolted into thoughts about death and widowhood when she hears about the death of a friend's husband. In this time of her life she may hear about many such deaths and begin to wonder if she will soon have to face widowhood herself. A husband may be beset with similar fears about himself as more of his contemporaries die.

The challenge here is to acknowledge these fears mutually, to share them and rationally deal with their implications. Your first inclination may be to push such thoughts out of your mind, because they are painful and anxiety-provoking. Besides, you want to protect your spouse from feeling alarm (Aren't there enough problems already?). But the thoughts will persist and demand to be discussed. Society today has acknowledged that death should not be considered a dirty little secret, as it once was. The media have taken this issue out of the closet and provided a stimulus for open family communication concerning the provisions that should be made prior to the death of a spouse. Will the wife be left adrift in a financial mess should the husband die first? Has a will been made, and are its provisions equitable? Is there enough life insurance and mortgage insurance and other income to afford a measure of economic security for her after his demise? Will she have to work outside the home, if she is not doing so now, to supplement her income? If so, what skills does she possess, and what skills might she need to obtain? What funeral arrangements (elaborate or modest, burial or cremation) need to be agreed upon? These questions are universal and require discussion in each family.

Raising and answering these questions will enable you to get on with living your life. Otherwise, your unspoken fears will haunt your mind and dim your view of the years ahead. The chances favor your having twenty to twenty-five years of vigorous life ahead. But the unexpected can happen long before that time, so provisions for the contingency of death require attention. Your emotional relief from anxiety is won through dealing with the problem of death rather than running away from it.

Similarly, the hopes, fears, and reservations you may have about retirement need to be surfaced for mutual discussion. Are you looking forward to retirement, or dreading it? You may be retiring from your job, but what will you retire to? Will freedom from the work routine mean freedom to do the things you've always wanted to do, or freedom to be bored? Will retirement mean the end of everything you value, or the beginning of something you can value more? Will retirement drive you and your spouse further apart (grating on each other's nerves from too much togetherness), or will you become closer by encouraging and reinforcing each other's drive to pursue individual activities and goals in addition to shared ones?

Preretirement discussions about these issues should be open-ended and ongoing, subject to changing circumstances. You are no longer required to retire at sixty-five; federal laws allow you to stay on at work past then. You may wish to think about continuing to work rather than retiring at sixty-five if you enjoy what you are doing or feel that it is the only economically feasible alternative you have. Or you may decide to take an earlier retirement in order to pursue new goals in life. The point is that all options should be kept open, with an understanding between you and your spouse that the final decisions both of you make about when or whether you retire, as well as your retirement objectives, are to be determined by the condition of your health, your marital relationship, your economic situation, and your outlook on life at the time.

## 7. The challenge to expand your view of yourself, your spouse, your family, and the world you live in.

After all these years, life has sent you the message, loud and clear, that nothing lasts forever. Everything ends—your youth, your early adulthood, your dreams of being rich and famous, your expectations regarding your spouse and children, your belief in the stability of our economic system and in the honesty of politicians, your sense of invulnerability to serious illness and death. Even the values you once held dear seem to have disappeared in today's social climate: the ideal of working for a purpose beyond immediate self-interest, peace in the world, dedication to religious good works, the notion of assuming personal responsibility for one's actions instead of blaming everyone else for what goes wrong, sacrifice and devotion to others, when needed, above selfish, instant gratification.

But there is another side to this coin: for every loss there is a gain. Your challenge is to identify those gains and use them as stepping stones to improving the present quality of your life. For example, when you "lose" your youth, you gain your mature years. You can approach your fifties as a time of opportunity, a time to experience something you have never experienced before.

What will it be like to live through your fifties? How will you react to good luck or adversity at this time in your life? Can you deal more constructively, skillfully, and effectively than you did before with the uncertainties life will present to you? Will you act courageously or fearfully under the pressures of a death in the family or losing your job?

Exploring these questions can make this time in your life a more enriching and interesting period than you ever suspected it could be. Instead of wallowing in "losing" your expectations about your spouse and your family, the challenge is to reexamine these expectations. Perhaps they were false or illusory in the first place. You might have expected your spouse to consider you the number one person in his or her life always because you believed that the marriage license guaranteed it. If you still believe this to be the case and are disappointed that your spouse no longer feels this way, then it's time for you to "lose" that belief and "gain" the knowledge that your relationship with your spouse cannot be taken for granted, and that you are an equal contributor to any alienation you may be experiencing in your relationship. Now would be the time to mutually explore the differences that separate you and understand each other in greater depth with a view toward bridging your separation gap.

If you have "lost" your expectations about your children, they may be well worth losing. You may be feeling self-righteous and complain about "that no good son of mine. After all we did for him, he's dropped out of college. I wanted him to be a lawyer like me, and instead he now says he wants none of it." Or your daughter may have just been divorced, and you are disappointed in her because you knew she was making a mistake by marrying the guy in the first place. In your estimation he was not "the right type" for her, and you know better than she does who the right type is. You expected her to follow your advice, but she didn't.

Now is the time to drop such expectations and self-righteousness about your children. In place of your sense of loss you can gain the knowledge that your children are now adults who have the right to live their own lives. For better or worse, they must take responsibility for their actions. You did the best you could to transmit to them the values, teachings, and behavior you thought were best for them when they were in your care as young children and adolescents. You gave them ground to stand on, but how they take flight from that ground is solely up to them. Respecting the individuality of your children and creating adult-to-adult relationships with them can prove to be an enriching gain at this time in your life.

"Losing" your belief that the people in government know best about how to run the country can become a gain in realism. It can make you aware that your active participation in the political process—working in concert with others holding beliefs similar to your own—will make for the improvements you desire. There are no "big daddies" in government; you can discover that you must be your own big daddy to make positive things happen.

The challenge to reaffirm your own integrity is implicit in these seeming "losses." Why should you run with the pack? If others are self-seeking, selfish, and guarded, you can demonstrate by your own actions that, by contrast, you primarily value caring and loving and openness. If others see no virtue in honesty, consideration, tact, and generosity, you can practice what they refuse even to preach. In doing so, you will gain a sense of self-worth by being your own person. There are more people in this country than you may suspect who feel as you do—and by acting on your beliefs you will find yourself drawing many of them to you.

The ultimate loss, the loss of your own life by dying, is in the offing. The poignant awareness of this may enable you to gain a greater sense of how precious each moment of life is and that now is the time to make the most of each moment. This is the time in life when you yourself may experience a life-threatening illness, such as a heart attack or a malignant tumor, and survive. As a consequence, you may gain an acute appreciation of the greatest gift you've been given, the gift of life itself. Here is your second chance to separate out the really important things from those you once thought were important in your life. In a sense, you have your life to live over, and perhaps you will discover the overriding importance of the simple things in life, as did Nadine Stair, eighty-five years old, of Louisville, Kentucky. But you may discover their importance long before she did. Here is what she discovered:

### If I Had My Life to Live Over

I'd dare to make more mistakes next time. I'd relax. I would limber up. I would be sillier than I have been this trip. I would take fewer things seriously. I would take more chances. I would take more trips. I would eat more ice cream and less beans. I would perhaps have more actual troubles, but I'd have fewer imaginary ones.

You see, I'm one of those people who live sensibly and sanely hour after hour, day after day. Oh, I've had my moments, and if I had it to do over again, I'd have more of them. In fact, I'd try to have nothing else. Just moments, one after another, instead of living so many years ahead of each day. I've been one of those persons who never goes anywhere without a thermometer, a hot water bottle, a raincoat, and a parachute. If I had it to do again, I would travel lighter than I have.

If I had my life to live over, I would start barefoot earlier in the spring and stay that way later in the fall. I would go to more dances. I would ride more merry-go-rounds. I would pick more daisies.

# Chapter Eight

# *The End-Is-the-Beginning Marriage*

The next-to-your-last marriage begins with an ending, the time of retirement (usually sixty-five), and will persist until one of you becomes a widow or widower, since it is quite rare for a couple to die at the same time.

The number sixty-five still strikes terror into people's hearts. This vision of sixty-five as the harbinger of senility and death continues to persist, even though it is false. It may have been more realistic in the early 1900s, when the average age at death for Americans was forty-seven. But, on the average, people now live well past their sixties. And with the help of modern medical science and psychological and holistic health practices they can live most of the rest of their days feeling alive and well. All the more reason, then, to fight society's stereotyping of sixty-five-year-olds as decrepit and irrelevant and to demonstrate by your own thoughts and actions that you are alive, well, and able to create new possibilities for yourself. This sixth marriage of your marriage can be a beginning, a retirement to a bright future as well as from a past business career.

No one in our society is exempt from traces of the negative stereotype of what "old age" is like. We recently experienced this reality personally at a seminar we gave. Alice, who is sixty-five, approached us during the coffee break and handed us a letter she said she had just received from an eighty-three-year-old friend who lives in a retirement home. She said she was touched by it and thought it might have some relevance to our discussion of age stereotypes. Here are the first three paragraphs of that letter:

Dear Folks:

I'm sure that the Bright Angel Retirement Home has thanked you and the many others who have made gifts to the home that has brought so much pleasure and comfort to us residents. But I wish to thank you personally from the bottom of my heart because I am the recipient of the little portable radio which you gave. I listen to it constantly while I am awake. I have never had a radio all my very own ever since I came to the home to live.

Everything is nice here and they take wonderful care of us. There are two of us in each room. My roommate is Martha Jenson. She is 87 and I am 83.

Martha has had a radio of her own ever since I came here ten years ago. She kept it so low I could never hear the programs. When I would ask her to turn it up so I could hear she wouldn't do it. Bless her. She is a sweet soul and I suppose she can't help being that way.

As we read those paragraphs, we were touched. What a nice, kindly, long-suffering old lady, we thought—just like in the movies. And then we read this last paragraph of the letter:

Last week she dropped her radio and it broke into so many pieces that it cannot be repaired. Last night I was

listening to the evening services of the First Methodist
Church and the beautiful old hymns that I love so well.
Martha asked me to turn it up so she could hear too. So
naturally I told her to go fuck herself.

Again thanking you, I am,

Gladys Gardiner

We laughed out loud. So much for stereotypes about "old"
people. We were reminded that the myth that all "very old"
women are sweet, kindly, self-effacing, and long-suffering dies
hard—our societal conditioning about the aged persists, even
when it clashes with reality.

We see what we have been conditioned to see. The last paragraph of the letter comes as a reality shock that tells us (if we're
listening) that "old" people are not what you may think they
are, but are unique individuals like anyone else and must be
judged as such. For every "sweet old lady" there is an irascible
one; for every "feisty old man" there is a passive one; for every
"helpless and hopeless old man or woman" there is one who
takes charge and is turned on to life; for every "passive, resigned
old man or woman" there is a political activist; for every "in-
tolerant, dogmatic old person" there is a tolerant, open-minded
one. For every "past-oriented, nostalgia-obsessed old-timer,"
there is one who is living in the present and is future-oriented.
All types are there in real life for us to see, if we wish to see them.
But we can see them only when we abandon our images of use-
lessness, senility, instant death, terminal disease, or virulent cancer
as the inevitable consequence of reaching a certain age.

If couples continue to allow themselves to believe that they
are society's throwaways, a black cloud of despair can overcome
them in this sixth marriage of their marriage. For this belief can
create a series of new triangles in their lives.

# The Typical Marriage Triangles of the End-Is-the-Beginning Marriage

## The Retirement-Disillusionment Triangle

The fantasy of a happy "golden years" retirement turns sour when it becomes a reality. The job you once held now becomes more valuable and significant after you left it, for the job not only meant pride in accomplishing a task and earning a paycheck, which validated your importance to society, it also meant a place to go where you were needed and wanted, where fellow workers became your friends, where you experienced a sense of community. By contrast, retirement has given you the "freedom" to become bored, purposeless, anxious, and depressed. A couple may discover that retirement creates a suffocating at-home togetherness that was nonexistent when they were subject to outside work schedules.

## The Despair Triangle

A husband and wife will make "friends" with their own despair if they feel their present life is a desert. They will nurture their bitterness and disappointment over life's indignities until they become an obsession. Buried beneath their bitterness and disappointment is unexpressed anger—anger that the better life they were "entitled" to was denied them; they were betrayed by circumstances. They apparently never realized that their births only entitled them to create their own positive circumstances or to react constructively to those circumstances beyond their control. Silent suffering, despondency, and depression are characteristics of this triangle, along with an excessive reliance on tranquilizers and liquor. Depression can take the form of increasing forgetfulness and helplessness, which are ways of wiping out the painful reality of their present life together. This is not the advent of so-called senility, but rather a protective guise designed to hide from themselves that their present and future are all one meaningless void.

### The Life-threatening-Illness Triangle

The illness triangle is more tangible than the despair triangle, because a specified illness is involved. Frequently it is a heart attack or cancer that becomes the "third party" in the relationship. A husband or a wife who experiences such a brink-of-death event and survives may subsequently react to that experience in either a positive or negative way. Those couples who have coped successfully with the challenges to their mutual development in their earlier marriages of their marriage will utilize that critical experience to grow closer together as a couple. They have received the warning that life may end at any time; therefore, they value what they have and are determined to make the most of the time they have left together.

# Your Mutual Development Challenges

1. **The challenge for you and your spouse to stretch yourselves and realize as much of your potential for happiness**

**and growth as is humanly possible during all the remaining years of your life together.**

To respond to this challenge constructively, you will first have to divest yourselves of traces of the negative thinking that says being sixty-five means becoming incapable of changing your life for the better. Dr. David Fischer offers some eloquent advice on this issue:

> The people who feel hopeless about being sixty-five
> are like the dog in the box with an electric grid on the
> bottom. You give him a shock, he runs for the door,
> can't make it, then to the window. He tries all kinds of
> things, but gets the shock no matter what he does. He
> can't escape that shock. Eventually all the dog does when
> you hit the buzzer that gives him the shock is stand there.
> Interesting thing: we open the door and hit the buzzer
> and the dog doesn't come out. You put a delicious meal
> on the other side of the door; we haven't fed him for
> days. He stands there. So we say the dog is psychotic.
> He's not psychotic. He's learned that no matter what
> he does, it doesn't work. He's learned hopelessness,
> that's what we have taught him, and that's what people
> are taught.

In the 1990s, most men and women sixty-five and over are vigorous, alert, intelligent, and active. Only 5 percent of all people over sixty-five are in nursing homes and convalescent hospitals, and their average age of admission is eighty, not sixty-five. You can overcome your "sixty-five is terror-time" age hangups when you recognize that your fear is unrealistic. There are positive role models everywhere who have discovered that sixty-five is a time for new beginnings. That observation can encourage you to make this time in your life a source of enrichment rather than despair.

Ted, a member of one of our seminars, is much more typical of today's sixty-five-year-old men and women than is commonly assumed. Here is what he has to say about the quality of his life:

"I just turned sixty-five last month. The surprise for me was that there was no surprise: I looked into my shaving mirror and found I wasn't twenty years older. The sky didn't fall on me, I didn't have a stroke or a heart attack, nor did I suddenly become bald. When I was thirty I thought sixty-five would make me ready for a nursing home, but I had just had my yearly medical checkup, and the doctor said I was in very good shape. My ticker is as good as it was ten years ago; I'm only five pounds overweight, and I'm working on that. I jog every morning, and eat balanced meals, and take some minerals and vitamins each day. I still play tennis on weekends, and my wife Terry and I go backpacking as often as we can. Sixty-five? It was just another day in my life. It wasn't the end of anything. I once thought it would mean I'd have to retire and that maybe that would be a good thing. But now I know I'll never retire, I'll always be active. My job turns me on too much. I switched my career at sixty and became an independent management consultant, and it's been a ball, let me tell you. I think I'm wiser, smarter than I ever was, and my long-term experience as an administrator makes me a damn good consultant. Oh, the one thing is different, now that I'm sixty-five—I'm less of a workaholic than I once was. My wife and I are doing more things together, so I'm getting to know her better. I see my two kids and my grandchildren more often. And smell the flowers more, instead of working until the late hours of the night. I figure, if I take care of my health and enjoy my work and my family and friends, I've got it made for at least another twenty years. The only thing I would change, if I could, would be to ask God to grant me much more time on earth than I have left. Good health and time. It's kind of sad, to know that I finally have so much knowledge about how to live a good life and can do so, that it will all end too soon. Because I feel more like a kid at the beginning of his career than a guy who's nearing the end."

The fact that Ted is healthy is not entirely an accident. He has taken personal responsibility for his physical condition for many years; it didn't happen that he is in good physical condition just because he wished for it. He got the best modern medical advice a long time ago about the need to exercise, about proper nutrition, about stress management, and applied it to himself. He has a full set of his own teeth because he prevented gum disease by twice-a-year visits to his dentist and proper brushing and flossing. He stopped smoking eighteen years ago and drinks in moderation. Consequently he can expect twenty more years of reasonably good health.

Ted's comments reveal that his chronological age is of no importance in determining his fate in life. He is much more concerned with his biological age—his physical and mental condition. It is up to him to continue to cultivate his mind and body through exercise and continued stress management.

The new adult age revolution has created tens of thousands of men and women who are experiencing their sixties in this positive way. You and your spouse have the opportunity to add to that number.

2. **The challenge to inform yourself with the latest factual knowledge about the physiological and psychological processes of aging, so you can act constructively at this time in your life.**

We are living in a changed world. Horror stories about aging are rapidly being supplanted by positive discoveries that have emerged from the medical, health, psychological, and social research of the past twenty-five years. Here are the key discoveries:

*a. Illness need not be a consequence of turning sixty-five.*
The way you take care of your body before sixty-five will determine how fit you will be in your post-sixty-five years. Your chronological age is not the causal factor: you are that factor at any age. The rock stars who died from heart attacks, drug overdoses, or depression in their twenties and thirties, Jimi Hendrix and Jim Morrison, for example, died at biological ages older than many people who are in their eighties. They had mercilessly abused their bodies and their minds and became "old" men while they were still in their early years chronologically. If you respect your body and appropriately care for it, you can expect your biological age to be at least ten years younger than your chronological one. Gerontologist James D. Manney, in an important study, *Aging and American Society* (published by the U.S. Department of Health, 1973), is explicit about the irrelevance, in fact, the danger, of equating advancing chronological age with illness:

> The judgment of chronological age is especially inaccurate in the case of older people . . . the biological and psychological processes of aging affect individuals at different rates and degrees. Even the most severe biological assaults —such as senile brain disease—affect behavior in an unpredictable way. Most of the age-related conditions will never appear in a given individual, or will not be serious enough to give him trouble. Others can be controlled by adequate medical care. Some of the individuals will be able to control themselves. Physical and psychological aging is not nearly as uniform as are our social expectations of older people.

*b. You do not become less intelligent and more forgetful and confused as you grow older.*
In fact, you become more intelligent, more acutely able to use all the experience you have accumulated in life—provided

you've been using your brain during your lifetime instead of transforming it into a huge television set. That old saying "Use it or lose it" applies equally well to your brain as to your car or your sexual capabilities.

The popularly held belief that because we lose thousands of brain cells as we grow older we must inevitably lose our wits by the time we are into our sixties is totally false. The lost brain cells are an infinitesimally small fraction of the billions upon billions of brain cells that never die. Whatever cell losses we may have are negligible in comparison to the cells that remain in functional order. Consequently these losses have absolutely no effect on the brain's ability to do its work.

The dreaded diseases of senile dementia and Alzheimer's, both of which disastrously affect mental and physical abilities, are in some ways age-connected, although they have occurred in persons much younger than sixty-five. In any case, 95 percent of people over sixty-five do not develop these diseases (and those who do are mostly over eight-five), so the odds are greatly in your favor.

Severe emotional depression is something you should be much more concerned about, because one out of five people over sixty-five suffer from it. This illness is not caused by your chronological age. (It is an illness that is also endemic among children, adolescents, and young and middle-aged adults.) It is a social, interpersonal illness caused by inappropriate psychological responses to devastating losses in life, such as the death of a loved one, loss of a job, a divorce, failure in business, and so on. In some cases depression is also caused by a biochemical imbalance. By means of psychological counseling and wise medication, intense depressive reactions can be overcome.

*c. You do not have to become a toothless old woman or a bent old man or deaf or blind just because you are now sixty-five.*

Your bones need not become brittle and weak with age, causing osteoporosis, which is a crippling disease that makes you vulnerable to fractures and stooped posture. Proper exercise can increase bone mineral content so that you can minimize this possibility. Reinforcing your bones in your earlier years is your best protection for later years. For postmenopausal women, Dr. Robert Butler has this recommendation: "We know there's a decisive drop in estrogens in postmenopausal women. We've discovered that the thinning of bones is partly a function of loss of estrogen. Therefore calcium intake is very important for women going through and beyond menopause."

Deafness and severe eyesight deterioration are not inevitable for people over sixty-five either. There are enormous variations in this age group, just as there are in people who are younger. Some loss of hearing and change in eyesight may require bifocal glasses in the later years, but the differences between individuals are far more significant than the similarities. It is commonly assumed that some deafness is inevitable as one ages, but there is new research to indicate that this might not be the case. For example, in primitive cultures, where the blasting noises that define a modern city are nonexistent, men and women in their seventies and eighties have been found with hearing ability as acute as that possessed by sixteen-year-olds in our society. There is now corrective surgery available for improving the sound conduction mechanism of the ear. For those who have lost their sensitivity to high frequency sounds, there are modern devices that can amplify them. Eye problems such as cataracts and detached retinas that were once thought uncorrectable are now corrected with laser surgery as a matter of course.

Similarly, there is no reason for you to lose your teeth. The major cause of tooth loss is gum (periodontal) disease, which is caused by bad diet and improper care of your teeth and gums, by not brushing and flossing with diligence and consistency. If your teeth need to be taken out in your sixties, you've paved the way for it in your twenties.

And your skin need not turn into a crinkled sheet of paper if you avoid becoming a suntan buff in your earlier years. Dr. Victor D. Newcomer, an expert dermatologist, is explicit on this point:

> What is generally referred to as aging, including the pebbly texture, the blotches and wrinkles on the skin, are by and large the result of excessive sun exposure down through the years. If you want to have good-textured skin in your later years, avoid needless and excessive exposure to the sun.

*d. You do not become a used-up, worn-out worker or career person just because you have turned sixty-five.*

If you wish to continue to work past sixty-five or seventy and are prevented from doing so, you are not the problem. The problem is the way our social, political, and business systems are currently organized. The committee on aging of the American Medical Association is very explicit on this topic:

> In view of progress, past and present, it is not unreasonable to expect a high percentage of those now 45 or 55 to be potentially valuable employees at 70 or 75 or even 80. If retirement is made flexible, the validity of the short job-tenure claim becomes extremely questionable. So, too, do many "pension problems."

Employers and labor should review their policies and attitudes in the light of current knowledge. Studies were conducted by the U.S. Department of Labor, Bureau of Employment Security, on the experience of firms hiring older workers. These firms described their older workers as follows:

1. They have the stability that comes with maturity.

2. Less time is wasted on the job by older workers.

3. They are more reliable and have a definite desire to work.

4. They have consistently less absenteeism and are more apt to stay on the job.

5. They have a sense of responsibility and loyalty to their job and their employer.

6. They generally have steady work habits and have a serious attitude toward their job.

7. They usually require less supervision once they are oriented on the job.

The AMA makes the further point that the creation of "useless" older people by means of chronological age discrimination is dangerous to society at large:

> For society, problems are created by failure to use the wisdom, experience and productivity of older persons. The void must be filled by the less capable. Instead of using older proficient people, society has to set up special agencies to care for them in their dependency. This not only is costly but would be needless if these persons were permitted to remain productive.
>
> Because of constant external and internal threats to our democratic way of life, misuse of our human resources can become a national disaster. It should not be forgotten that our older citizens were called upon to preserve and build our way of life. They should not be denied the fruits of freedom, including the right to work.
>
> If unrealistic policies of employment and retirement are continued, a long step may be taken toward creation of a special class, resentful of its loss of status and clamoring for preferential treatment at the expense of the rest of society. The dangers inherent in such segregation obvi-

ously will be increased as the continuing revolution
in aging adds untold numbers to this segment of the
population.

This large group, armed with the vote, may through
governmental action, succeed in procuring an inequitable
share of the nation's goods even though its initial purpose
is only defense of itself. Such inequities could produce
serious conflicts between this group and the younger
members of society who pay the bill. The myriad social
consequences of such a conflict could be highly detrimental to the entire population. There is no action more
important in the new era of aging, from the standpoint of
social, economic and health needs, than the elimination
of job discrimination based on chronological age.

*e. Your mental attitude about being sixty-five makes the dif-
ference between being fully alive or two-thirds dead at that age.*

If you believe your life is over at sixty-five, it will be. You
will have created a self-fulfilling prophecy. Stories of people
who have strokes or heart attacks and die just before their sixty-
fifth birthdays, or shortly after their retirement at that age, are,
unfortunately, all too true. Panic reactions resulting from a belief that life is over at sixty-five have done their lethal work.

Why a person engages in such self-defeating behavior is
perceptively analyzed by Leonard C. Lewin in his book *Triage*
(New York: The Dial Press, 1972, p. 211): "People tend to do
what they *assume* is expected of them, however unacceptable
their actions may appear, even to themselves, at sufficient distance in time. And they readily learn to accept—as normal—the
actions of others that can be justified only by assigning prime
value to adaption to things as they are *assumed* to be . . ."

By contrast, if you regard being sixty-five as a challenge
to live the latter part of life to the fullest degree, to see the

possibilities that inhere in each new day, you will remain "youthful" regardless of your chronological age.

Dr. Marian Diamond, a brain research authority points out, "Our attitudes are depicted in our total body structure. We've made gray hair a negative. When you tell people they're getting old, make them withdraw from society and the positive feedback we all need, then they really begin to age. If we turned it around, made gray hair and wrinkles signs of character and experience, a positive event, that would affect the brain, which in turn would affect the aging process."

However, you don't have to wait until society's attitudes change. If you have a positive self-image, a good measure of self-esteem about your competencies and abilities as a human being without regard to your chronological age, that fact in and of itself enables you to experience the years over sixty-five in a satisfying way, even in the face of stressful new occurrences.

For it is in these later years that a large number of losses in life may happen (they can also happen in earlier years, but usually in less significant numbers): the loss of the status role of the job holder through retirement, the loss of a spouse who dies, the loss of health, the loss of relatives and friends who die. A stunning series of such blows may accumulate over a relatively short period. The emotional trauma of such events may lead to mental depression, which is one of the most widespread illnesses among people over sixty-five. It is also a great killer, for to be severely depressed is to give up on life, to lose the will to live. It is a way of willing oneself to die, which can create death. This phenomenon can be observed in the depressed men and women who are forced into nursing homes against their will. They view this as a death sentence, and often die after just one to three months, even though their physical conditions would have indicated that they had many years of life left in them.

Research in the new medical-psychological field of psycho-neural immunology reveals that the emotions of hopelessness, helplessness, powerlessness, and despair, felt in an acute form by a person who is experiencing the blows of fate, negatively affects the body's immune system. The person who does not cope constructively with these traumatic events will lower his or her resistance to physical illness. The body's ability to ward off viral infections, pneumonia, heart attack, strokes, and perhaps cancer may be severely impaired.

The alternative is to mourn these severe losses and recognize that your loved ones who have died still live inside you in the way they enriched your life. Because they are no longer a part of this world, the goal is now to reach out and make new friends and possibly find new lovers. They will never supplant these loved ones, but they can be supplements that can enrich your life in the present.

If your entire personal identity was wrapped up in your status as a working person, the loss of that status can leave you desolate. The alternative is to reappraise the meaning of "success" and "failure" and to let go of the belief that you were only your job. Success as a fully human being means more than working at a job and making money. It means being a caring, loving person, a dedicated spouse and nurturing parent, a concerned citizen involved in the issues in your community, the nation, and the world. And if your retirement has proved disappointing, the alternative is to use your intelligence to create a new job for yourself or to become involved in a political or social organization or in an absorbing hobby that will shore up your sliding self-image.

Even in the extreme case of terminal illness, you still have a choice about how you will experience your dying. You can still experience personal growth by recognizing and accepting that death, in Rabindranath Tagore's words, "belongs to life as birth does, even as walking contains the raising of the foot as much as the laying of it down."

Dr. Irvin Yalom has worked for many years with terminally ill cancer patients and writes, in *Existential Psychotherapy* (New York: Basic Books, 1980):

> I have been struck by how many of them use their crisis and their danger as an opportunity for change. They report startling shifts, inner changes that can be characterized in no other way than personal growth:
>
> - A rearrangement of life's priorities: a trivializing of the trivial.
>
> - A sense of liberation: being able to choose not to do those things they do not wish to do.
>
> - An enhanced sense of living in the immediate present, rather than postponing life until retirement or some other point in the future.
>
> - A vivid appreciation of the elemental facts of life: the changing seasons, the wind, falling leaves, the last Christmas, and so forth.
>
> - Deeper communication with loved ones than before the crisis.
>
> - Fewer interpersonal fears, less concern about rejection, greater willingness to take risks, than before the crisis.

These findings confirm that we are truly living in the presence of an emerging adult age revolution. One of the most significant conclusions you can draw from these five revolutionary discoveries of modern medical science about the aging process is that your own chronological age is irrelevant, even dangerous, if you use it as the sole indicator of who you are as a whole person or of what you may become. These discoveries shift responsibility for the direction your life is taking from something external (your chronological age, which you can't do anything about) to you, something you can do something about. In today's world, the choice is up to you.

### 3. The challenge to affirm the meaningfulness and richness of your past and present life together.

The ultimate, undeniable reality at sixty-five is the reality that you will die. It will happen to both of you, if not soon, then probably within the next two decades, which will fly by as fast as the previous decades have flown. However, the acute awareness of your own mortality can prove positive, because it can serve as an incentive for the two of you to review your marital life history, which will reaffirm the meaningfulness of your lives. You will find much, much more of value in your life together than you were aware of during the many trying periods in your marital relationship. Did you really have a relationship? No, you had *many* relationships with each other.

You were the passionate romantic lovers who took out your marriage license—and had to learn that nobody lives happily ever after. You were mother and father to each other—and had to learn not to act like demanding, helpless children in response to the mother or father image you imposed on yourselves. You were two abandoned infants acting fearfully toward each other when faced with unemployment or the death of a parent—and had to learn you only felt like helpless infants but were in fact adults who had the inner strength and capacity to weather these blows of fate. You were greedy children when you were denied the instant gratification from your spouse that you felt you were entitled to—and had to learn the value of treating each other as separate adults whose needs might not always coincide.

You were rivals in a power struggle over who ran the household—and had to learn the virtue of shared family responsibilities freely undertaken, because there is no master or slave in a good marital relationship. You were two manipulators who attained your ends indirectly by sulking, pouting, withdrawing, or withholding—and had to learn that open communication, shared feelings, and kindly discussions worked infinitely better as ways of resolving problems. You were jealous rivals, jealous of the love your spouse lavished on his or her parents or on your own children—and had to learn that such love was not a denial of adult love to one's spouse, but was an expression of filial devotion and parental love that was never meant to be viewed as rejection of your spouse.

You were business competitors, viewing your spouse's larger paycheck as evidence of your own lack of worthiness—and had to learn that your self-image did not depend on what you earned but on the qualities you possessed as a human being. You were cold acquaintances to each other when you sensed another man or woman in the picture—and had to learn that your spouse was issuing a cry for help, wanting the marriage partner to become a more interesting, lively, and attractive person and, failing that, looked elsewhere. You were preteen children when you related to your parents—and had to learn to assert yourselves and demonstrate that you were adults who had the right to live your own lives and make your own major decisions without well-intentioned interference from parents who always thought they knew what was best. You were a togetherness-at-all-times couple—and had to learn that you could love each other by respecting the differences between you as well as the similarities. You were rigid parents who tried to make your children into your own images, and quarreled over which of those images should predominate—but had to learn that your children were persons in their own right and therefore would determine their own fate once they left the nest.

Yes, you've learned more than you realized. What once seemed like random, isolated events in your life together now seem to have had a purpose. The purpose was to make you grow as individuals and as a couple. And you could only do so by divesting yourselves of your illusions and substituting constructive realities in their place. The many relationships you had with each other turned into strands that meshed into the making of the paramount relationship that lasts throughout one's lifetime—the two-gether marriage relationship. For the trials and tribulations of the past turned you into two adults who know that interdependency, separateness, and togetherness harmonize with one another into a good marriage, that when two separate people continue to grow, the marital relationship continues to grow.

By developing your capabilities, you have attained wisdom, although you may be hesitant to call it by that name. But that, indeed, is your real achievement. Wisdom is not a quality designed for a tiny elite but is available for everyone to work toward and achieve. The dictionary defines wisdom as an "understanding of what is true, right, or lasting." You have discovered that only love is lasting—love of one's spouse, one's children, one's parents, the world in which all persons are brothers and sisters, and the spiritual love that reveals that all of us are connected with something much greater than ourselves in the universe. You understand that what is true is being true to yourself: to act with integrity, to eliminate self-deception, to be courageous and take risks when the situation requires, to think for yourself rather than delegate the thinking to others, to relate to people out of the strength that love elicits rather than out of anger, which is weakness. You also have understood what is right: a belief in the abiding values of family life and a realization that life is an affair of people rather than things.

Looking back, couples such as you can take comfort in seeing that your life together turned out rather well after all. Many times in the past it did not seem that way. But the children turned out surprisingly well. The values, love, and attention you gave them in the critical early years of their lives did pay off after all. It took longer than you had hoped for, but they are in effective charge of their own lives now. You've made your peace with your own parents. You can forgive them for the errors they made in your upbringing and value what they did right, instead of wrong, during the time you lived with them. And you hope your children will give you that same understanding as they grow older.

Now that you have mellowed, both of you can forgive yourselves for errors of omission and commission done to your family, because they arose from unawareness rather than intent. You'll become infallible only when you become saints. Both of you have provided a measure of economic security for your family by working hard all those many years. Your work contributed to the wealth and strength of the economy. You've tried to influence the shape of society by participating in political activity and standing up for what you believe in. If it all hasn't turned out to be to your liking, you can feel validated because you did the best you could as individuals. You tried and can honor yourselves for that fact.

Was it all worthwhile? Your life review has answered the question.

There is, however, one last marriage of your marriage: the after-death marriage, which is the stage when you become a widow or widower. For, with the exception of an accident or mutual suicide, couples die separately, at different times. When this happens, the remaining spouse will face the ultimate triangles and challenge that life will create for you.

# Chapter Nine

# *The After-Death Marriage*

Because death is an inevitable part of life, this seventh marriage of your marriage ends with the death of your spouse, when you become a widow or widower. Because on the average women live eight years longer than men, 75 percent of all currently married women are liable to be widowed at some time in life. As we previously noted, you and your spouse are quite likely to live for ten to twenty more productive years once you reach sixty-five. But just as life has a beginning, it also has an end.

But does a marriage really end with the death of a spouse? Though a physical ending certainly takes place, the lived experience of a lifetime of partnership doesn't end with physical death. That lived experience remains very much alive in the person who lives on. Your spouse is now spirit rather than a physical entity, but that spirit remains "married" to you until you yourself become spirit. If you do not deal constructively with the physical death of your spouse, the rest of your own days may be haunted by two triangles; the effect of either is to cause you to die while you still live, rather than living until you die.

# The Typical Marriage Triangles of the After-Death Marriage

### The I'm-Still-Married-to-My-Dead-Spouse Triangle

If you feel that your spouse never died and that he or she is constantly observing your everyday activities, you are experiencing the I'm-still-married-to-my-dead-spouse triangle. He or she is "there" when you date or even ask an acquaintance of the opposite sex out for lunch or dinner. You then feel you are being judged and found wanting, unfaithful to your spouse even though he or she is dead. If this triangle is not constructively eliminated from your life, seclusion, isolation, and reclusiveness will characterize your remaining years.

### The Guilt-Is-Now-My-Life-Partner Triangle

If you accuse yourself for not dying first and feel guilty because you, rather than your spouse, are still alive, you are making guilt your life partner. You have mixed feelings: resentment because you have been "betrayed" by your spouse's death, hurt at having been deprived of his or her companionship and nurturing. Bitterness, regret, and wallowing in despair are the consequences of this triangle.

## *Your Ultimate Challenge*

The ultimate challenge of this last marriage of your marriage is the challenge to make the most of your remaining years should your spouse die first. Fate will deal the cards that announce the timing of your spouse's death and your own death, but the quality of your life together today, and of the separate life you may be forced to lead in the future, will be determined by your reaction to the cards you are dealt.

Under even the best of circumstances, you will feel loneliness, grief, anger, and despair when your spouse dies. If it is quick and unexpected, your spouse will have been spared the agony of a lengthy illness. There is bitter comfort in that fact, but it can lessen your own pain.

Should it be otherwise, should your spouse die after a long illness, the capacity for fortitude and courage in both may be tested to the hilt. In the process of being a caring companion to your spouse during this anguishing period, you share suffering that can also become the ultimate affirmation of your love for each other—an epiphany that confirms the choice you made when you married your partner. The life you led together was indeed worthwhile.

Your spouse, though departed from this world, never dies. He or she continues to live in your heart, mind, and soul as long as you live. Your spouse's image, thoughts, feelings, actions, wisdom, and love for you now abide inside you. The memories of your mutual struggles and triumphs over adversity, your mutual joys and pleasures, your mutual achievements, are the legacy your spouse has left you. They will prove comforting in your darkest hours.

Once your period of mourning over your spouse's demise ends (mourning is both necessary and healthy and varies considerably from person to person in its duration), you may feel the urge to seek out new companionship with the opposite sex—and feel very guilty about it. You may find yourself thinking, "I will be betraying my spouse if I act on my sexual desires. I really am an unfaithful SOB for having any sexual feelings at all. How can I be happy with someone else, when my spouse is in the grave?" And when you do date, you may create a triangle, with the memory of your spouse playing third person. You may repeatedly call your new friend by your spouse's name or compare his or her actions, speech, and presence with your spouse's, finding the new person flawed in all these respects. You may see those deficiencies in every person of the opposite sex you meet, and in so doing, you may find yourself sexually inhibited or even impotent. That may well surprise and disturb you, because you never had such problems with your spouse.

All these problems arise out of an unrealistic belief that attaining companionship and love with people of the opposite sex (possibly including marriage) would be a betrayal of your deceased spouse. Out of feelings of guilt for being alive, all too many widows and widowers assume the burden of permanent penitence for their "sin" of having outlived their loved one. The challenge that confronts you is to come to terms with these guilt feelings, to recognize that the guilt is unnecessary, unproductive, and of no benefit whatsoever to your deceased spouse. Your spouse now lives as spirit, while you are still a physical human being possessed of all the drives and emotions the flesh is heir to. If your spouse were to return to earth, he or she would be distressed over the way you are punishing yourself. He or she would want you to be as happy and fulfilled as you possibly can be while you are in your physical form. Your lifelong penitence can have no affect on him or her because you two no longer live in the same worlds.

Of course, no new person can take your spouse's place. Your spouse enlarged your capacity to love and to enjoy life. You can utilize that capacity now with someone else in ways that can enliven your remaining years. The love and companionship you have with someone else will be different from that which you had with your spouse. But it can be sustaining and satisfying in its own right. Your deceased spouse gave you the gift of love, which was not meant to be destroyed by his or her death. It is a fact that marriages among widows and widowers over sixty-five are increasing by thousands each year. By marrying again, surviving partners are paying tribute to their spouse's memory, not defiling it.

As long as you remain alive, life offers you the supreme invitation to live. That is the ultimate challenge to the despair created by the death of your loved one. Walt Whitman's beautiful words in his "Song of Myself" celebrate the triumph over that despair:

All goes onward and outward, nothing collapses,
And to die is different from what any one supposed, and
   luckier . . .
They are alive and well somewhere,
The smallest sprout shows there is really no death,
And if there ever was, it led forward life, and does not
wait at the end to arrest it,
And ceas'd the moment life appear'd.

Here are two people we have worked with who have dealt with the death of a spouse in this constructive way. They have something important to say to all of us.

### Brian's Story

"I was 66 when my wife Ellen died suddenly at sixty-two—a heart attack, first time, over and out. Ellen was such a healthy woman, and we had planned, two months before she died, to go to Ireland to visit my relatives. It was something we had wanted to do for ten years, but by the time we would have gotten around to it, she was gone.

"We had everything going for us—my photocopying business was thriving, so I could work less because I didn't want to retire—but now it was all meaningless because she was gone. A good marriage of thirty-five years and now this big hole in my life. A black pit, that's what my life was like during that first year after her death. My kids were on their own, three thousand miles away, and I isolated myself from everyone. I was killing a fifth of scotch a day to blank out everything.

"I think there's a self-healing process at work in everyone who has a terrible experience like the death of Ellen, because after a year of almost destroying myself physically and mentally (always thinking, Why did she have to go first, why couldn't it have been me?) it suddenly dawned on me that Ellen, wherever she is in heaven, was looking at me and saying, 'You're still living on this earth, so make the best contribution you can while you're still there. Celebrate the life we had together by keeping connected with others instead of destroying yourself with self-pity.'

"That was four years ago. I'm seventy now, but happy with the legacy Ellen left me. She was always volunteering, helping others—the cancer foundation, mental health association, abused-wives centers—you name it. She did it joyously, happily. And I knew that's what she wanted me to do—to give of myself freely, to help others less fortunate than I. And because the business world felt like dust in my throat now that I was without her, I thought, why not—I'll work with the homeless, because they were getting such a rotten deal from society. And that's what I've been doing through my church. It's been gratifying, fulfilling work—reaching out to others and helping them. My marrying again? No, I don't feel that way. In a sense I feel married to the world, more connected than I ever was. That's enough for me. It's not that I would feel unfaithful to Ellen to marry again, it's just that my need at this time in my life is for the spiritual fulfillment of doing what I can for others who desperately need help."

### Eve's Story

"John died five years ago. It was cancer of the liver, a slow, agonizing death. At first I was out of my mind. I never knew that life could be so cruel and that I could feel depths of pain that seemed to go on forever. I felt my life was over. Friends would try to comfort me, but gave up because I had no desire to live. Yes, I thought of suicide, but my religion prevented me from taking my own life. I was sixty-two at the time (John died when he was sixty-seven).

"All that changed two years after his death, when I had an epiphany—you know, a sudden insight that my life wasn't over yet, that positive things could still happen. That epiphany took the form of a birthday party my childhood friend Beth insisted I come to; she would take no excuses from me. I went in spite of myself; now looking back I think God was pushing me toward it.

"I was surprised to find that half of the fifty-six people present were older than I was, and ranged in age from sixty-eight to eighty. I had never met any of these older people before and was surprised to learn of their wide-ranging interests and activities. They were so alive—the alertness of their minds, the interesting talk, the intensity with which they voiced their convictions, the spontaneity of their laughter all testified to that fact. I felt so comfortable in their presence, because they seemed devoid of any of the pretense, the phoniness, the need to always be on stage that infect younger people. They were at ease with themselves, so that they enabled people to be at ease with them.

"I made the mistake of asking one man in his early seventies if he was retired, and he looked surprised. No, he was a self-employed appraiser who still worked at his job but took one day off from work each week to paint in the park. Another man in his late sixties was a consultant on retirement planning who still had a substantial business practice. There was a retired newspaper reporter who was working on a novel; a pixielike piano tuner, certainly older than sixty-five, who spent time training younger persons in his business. The senior person present was an eighty-year-old man with an arthritic condition who was engaged in tape-recording the history of his life and times as a gift to his grandchildren. I later learned that the consultant on retirement plans had had three heart attacks in the past seven years, but you would never know it from his attitude toward life.

"I had expected most of the women present to be housewives and nothing else. My biggest surprise was that all of them were involved in some business or community-service activity. There were retired teachers who were now working in political organizations like NOW and the Gray Panthers. There was a CPA, a lawyer, a psychologist, and a social worker. All of them were over sixty-five, and the social worker and the lawyer were in their seventies. Most of them had been widowed! Yet here they were—bright, lively, alert, and concerned about the world we live in, instead of feeling pity for themselves as I was doing.

"After leaving the party I felt ashamed of myself. I had mourned long enough. I knew I had because I took the names, addresses, and phone numbers of the women who appealed to me. It was only a few days later that I began to get in touch with them (I surprised myself, because I reached out to them instead of doing nothing). Janet, the social worker, urged me to go back to school and get a master's degree in public health, a field I was always interested in. I expressed fear I couldn't make it because

I was too old. She laughed and said, 'Don't be silly, I got my social work master's when I was sixty-eight, so you can too!' She was right. I applied at my local college, was accepted, and graduated a year ago. I'm now a public health educator and loving every minute of my job. As for marriage again, well, there is a man of my age, a director of an AIDS clinic, who 'dates' me (my, that's an old-fashioned word!). He, too, lost a partner. It's just companionship now. It feels nice. The piece of paper that's a marriage license isn't important. What is important is that we value our companionship. So we'll see."

A year later we received an invitation to their wedding.

And what about your inevitable latter-day confrontation with your own death? There is realistic comfort in believing we are all transformed into spirit—the spirit that your dead spouse now possesses and that will eventually possess you. We become not "nothing," but "no-thing." The great poet Bertolt Brecht expressed this beautifully in a poem he wrote on his deathbed at the Charité hospital. Here is his homage to his physical disappearance from this earth:

### When in My White Room at the Charité

When in my white room at the Charité
I woke towards morning and heard the
Blackbird, I understood better.
I had lost all fear of death. For
Nothing can be wrong with me if I myself
Am nothing. Now I managed to enjoy
The song of every blackbird after me too.

# The Two-gether Dance of Marriage

⊱════⊰

The other night we saw an old Ginger Rogers and Fred Astaire movie called *Top Hat* on TV, and it was as though we were seeing them dance for the very first time, even though we had seen all their pictures years ago. We remembered them as a dance "team," which meant Fred always held Ginger closely, always led her in the direction he wanted to go: they were two soul mates clinging together blissfully, two hearts beating as one as they floated along the dance floor. At twenty-one, our eyes drank in the romance of it all, particularly when they danced a number called "Cheek to Cheek."

The other night, however, we saw a different dance team. Their names were Ginger Rogers and Fred Astaire, and they were dancing the "Cheek to Cheek" number—but it wasn't the same number we remembered seeing before. Ginger and Fred don't dance "check to cheek" most of the time as they move across the dance floor. Fred holds Ginger lightly, and Ginger doesn't cling to him as if he were her lifeline. He doesn't direct her every move. To the contrary, they frequently let each other move in opposite directions, and Ginger's dance steps differ from Fred's rather than duplicating them when they separate. Apart from each other, they give full expression to their individual reactions to the music, but they are always aware that they eventually will return to each other. And when they do, they merge affectionately and dance joyously together in the same direction as if in acknowledgment that their separate identities validate their togetherness. They hold each other freely, neither forcing the other. There's no boredom in their dance, for they do the unexpected; they play against the rhythm of the music at times, and at other times they syncopate their steps rather than moving in lockstep to the repetitiveness of the rhythm of the music. There is mutual respect for each other in the way they dance. When they break away from each other during the number, they do so confident that both of them will perform well on their own. Their timing is perfect—they know when to come together and when to let go.

Watching this "new" version of that old dance, we both had the same thought, "Yes, of course, Ginger and Fred are dancing the 'two-gether marriage'!" When we were twenty-one, we saw in that "Cheek to Cheek" dance an image of togetherness forever, with the woman clinging to the man, who would direct all the dance steps in her life and make her happy. Now we see the dance for what it really was: two people secure in themselves who dance together because the dance allows them the freedom to be themselves as well as part of a couple and enables them to make of that fact a joyous event. It is the "two-gether" dance of marriage: two equal people delighting in their equality and in their interdependence, a relationship designed to ensure a lifetime of love and happiness.

# Index

We welcome your response to our book, as we wrote it with the objective of helping everyone desiring long-term happiness in a committed relationship.

Please feel free to write us about your interpersonal relationship concerns. We continue to work with individuals and couples who wish to improve their relationships and can be reached at:

Creative Divorce, Love & Marriage Counseling Center
P.O. Box 150162
San Rafael, CA 94915